CHRISTMAS WITH STEPHEN LEACOCK

REFLECTIONS ON THE YULETIDE SEASON

NATURAL HERITAGE/NATURAL HISTORY INC.
TORONTO, ONTARIO

I once asked a Christmas eve group of children if they believed in Santa Claus. The very smallest ones answered without hesitation, "Why, of course!" The older ones shook their heads. The little girls smiled sadly but said nothing. One future scientist asserted boldly, "I know who it is"; and a little opportunist with his eye on gain said: "I believe in it all; I can believe in anything." That boy, I realized, would one day be a bishop.

— from "War-Time Santa Claus"

Canadian Cataloguing in Publication Data

Leacock, Stephen, 1869-1944
    Christmas with Stephen Leacock

ISBN 0-920474-47-0

1. Christmas - Humor. I. Title.

PS8523.E15C48 1988 C818'.5207 C88-095425-6
PR9199.2.L42C48 1988

Cover Photo:
Leacock in winter attire about 1928.
(Courtesy of the Public Archives of Canada)

Christmas with Stephen Leacock
Published by Natural Heritage/Natural History Inc.
P.O. Box 69, Postal Station H
Toronto, Ontario
M4C 5H7
Copyright © November 1988

Design: Derek Chung Tiam Fook
Text Production: Robin Brass Studio
Printed and bound in Canada by
T.H. Best Printing Company Limited

A SELECTED BIBLIOGRAPHY

PUBLISHED

The following stories have appeared in the
publications named:
"Christmas Rapture," *My Remarkable Uncle*,
McClelland & Stewart, 1968.
"Merry Christmas," *Frenzied Fiction*, McClelland
& Stewart, 1965.
"This Merry Christmas," printed as "A Christmas
Star Shines Through the Mists" in the *New York
Times Magazine*, December 25, 1938.
"Christmas Fiction and National Friction," *The
Spectator*, November 18, 1932.
"Hoodoo McFiggin's Christmas," *Literary Lapses*,
McClelland & Stewart, 1957.
"A Christmas Examination," *College Days*, The
Mayflower Press, Wm. Bredon and Son, 1923.
"A Christmas Letter," *Literary Lapses*, McClelland & Stewart, 1957.
"Caroline's Christmas," *Laugh with Leacock*,
McClelland & Stewart, 1968.
"The Errors of Santa Claus," *Frenzied Fiction*,
McClelland & Stewart, 1965.
"The Christmas Ghost," *Winnowed Wisdom*,
McClelland & Stewart, 1971.
"War-Time Santa Claus," *My Remarkable Uncle*,
McClelland & Stewart, 1968.
"War-Time Christmas," *My Remarkable Uncle*,
McClelland & Stewart, 1968.
"Scenes from a Renovated Christmas," *National
Home Monthly*, December 1935.

UNPUBLISHED

"Let Us Be Thankful," "First Aid to the Christmas Tourist," "Merry Christmas, Mars," "A
Blighted Christmas," and "This Discoloured
Christmas."

CONTENTS

THE AUTHOR

Stephen Leacock was born in 1869 at Swanmore in Hampshire, England. In 1876 the family emigrated to Canada and settled on a farm near Lake Simcoe. Educated at Upper Canada College and the University of Toronto, Stephen Leacock taught first at his old school of Upper Canada and later at McGill University in Montreal, where he rose to be head of the department of economics and political science. His first writings dealt with economics and Canadian history, but gradually as his true genius emerged he grew further and further away from this field and was attracted into his natural element of pure fun. Now he is remembered mainly as a humourist and the author of close to forty books of nonsense, including Literary Lapses, Nonsense Novels, Sunshine Sketches of a Little Town, Behind the Beyond, Moonbeams From the Larger Lunacy, Frenzied Fiction, Short Circuits, Helements of Hickonomics, Our British Empire, Over the Footlights, and Arcadian Adventures with the Idle Rich. At the time of his death in 1944, Leacock left four completed chapters of what was to have been his autobiography. These were published posthumously under the title The Boy I Left Behind Me. In 1946 it was decided by the Leacock Society to present a silver medal annually to the best book of humour published in Canada during the year. The Leacock Medal has become one of the outstanding awards in the literary world.

INTRODUCTION

A new book from Stephen Leacock for Christmas! How pleased he would be. The situation would seem fitting to his literary career - for Leacock was a pro.

Because he retained his professorship at McGill University in Political Economy, there has been a kind of silent conspiracy among critics and readers to consider Stephen Leacock a gifted amateur. He did not give up medicine like Somerset Maugham to write. He did not abandon law like Washington Irving to woo a literary mistress. Instead, more like Oliver Wendell Holmes, he stayed in one of the real professions - one which required certification on paper, real degrees - and turned out his "little pieces on the side."

But Leacock knew that his income from his writing every year brought him from four to eight times his academic salary. McGill never paid him more than $5000, but in his best year - 1927 when he built his nineteen room retreat at Old Brewery Bay for $2700 - he made $40,000 with his pen.

Oh, he knew he was a pro. He wrote his agent one time, "Let me know ahead of time how much you want and I can write it to the syllable." (One thinks of Trollope writing 1500 words each morning.)

Funny men always have to pretend that their stuff is spontaneous. "A funny thing happened to me on the way to the theater." This gives the illusion that humour is not a profession but a mysterious sixth sense. No doubt humorists have to have a special talent for seeing the world, but even the seeing is hard work. In *How To Write* Leacock said "Writing is no trouble. You just jot down things as they occur to you. Sometimes the occurring gives you some trouble." Of course the "occurring" is where the real problem lies. All professional writers know that.

Other clearly professional humorists paid Leacock the compliment of treating him as one of themselves and learning from him. Robert Benchley once wrote, "I have enjoyed Leacock's work so much that I have written everything he ever wrote - anywhere from one to five years after him." Chic Sale maintained a long-running friendship and visited at Old Brewery Bay. S. J. Perelman acknowledged his debt to the Canadian master. To see Leacock's place in his profession, one has only to read, at the beginning of *Laugh with Leacock*, the long list of humorists who wanted to express their gratitude and admiration.

One mark of the professional for Leacock was to write for the trade. He always tried to catch the Christmas season with his new book each year. The professional whom he most admired, Charles Dickens, had regularly had a Christmas story ready for the journals. Hoodoo McFiggin is probably as close as Leacock ever came to writing his own Tiny Tim. He inordinately coveted Dicken's ability to make his readers cry as well as laugh in the same story. (It is said that clowns always want to play Hamlet.) He knew, however, his own limitations and did not attempt the pathos he liked so in Dickens. But he did try to have his own Christmas material ready on time. Stephen Leacock saw this timing as part of his responsibility to his publishers and his readers.

The range of this book spans virtually all of Stephen Leacock's writing career. The earliest piece came with his first book, *Literary Lapses*, in 1910. Others are scattered through his canon until the last, "War-Time Christmas," appeared in *My Remarkable Uncle* in 1942. Readers will find favourites - like "The Errors of Santa Claus" - which will recall their joy at first reading. But it is to be hoped, too, that they will find at least one piece which will give them that fresh joy now.

Despite the limited subject of the holiday, the pieces in this book are a rather good representation of Leacock's work. Some of the sketches are purely funny; their whole purpose is entertainment. Some of them are more serious in their intent; they bring his academic expertise to bear on social or political problems of the time. Even these latter pieces are shot through with his inimitable humour. But this range, itself, shows his professionalism. The "funny" ones were certainly written "on speculation" - written with the hope that some editor would want them. The more "serious" essays were probably written at the express invitation of the market. It was not unusual for the *New York Times* to request commentary from Leacock at timely intervals. And he never disappointed them.

He was a pro - a real pro.

Prof. Ralph L. Curry
Chairman, English Department
Georgetown College
Georgetown, Kentucky

If I could talk to any one in Canadian history, it would be Stephen Leacock. Wouldn't it be wonderful to sit around the fireplace on a wintry night and listen to him tell a story?

Oh, you can have your famous politicians, business tycoons and the like. I'd take Stephen Leacock because he would make me laugh. I cannot imagine him without hearing laughter at the same time.

Unfortunately, it is not possible to have the real Stephen Leacock in person but we do have the next best thing - his stories.

So read on, and listen carefully. If the wind doesn't howl too loud, perhaps you'll hear the chuckle of an old man reading in a boat house overlooking Old Brewery Bay.

— Gary Lautens

12

CHRISTMAS RAPTURE

PRE-WAR

Well, well, here's Christmas time again, and Christmas almost here! There's always a sort of excitement as it gets near, isn't there? Only this morning the postman was saying - there's a genial fellow, if you like, that postman - was saying that Christmas is right on top of us. I said, not yet, but he said, oh yes, as good as here. He said it was real Christmas weather, too. I thought, not yet, but he insisted. He said that why he likes Christmas is that he has three kiddies, all boys. He always takes them out on Christmas. My! I hope he takes them a good long way this Christmas! Japan, eh?

The furnace man was talking too. He says I'll be having company round Christmas and so he's going to drive the furnace a bit. I tell him I don't expect much company, but he says he is going to coax her along anyway. The furnace man comes from the old country and where he worked, the gentleman he worked for - this, of course, was a real gentleman - used to give him a goose every Christmas. Never missed. That was nice, wasn't it. The furnace man has four kiddies, all boys; he says it's a great business for him and the missus thinking what to give them all... I do hope they can think of something good this year.

But, as I say, as Christmas gets near there's a sort of excitement about it. Such a lot of things to go to - concerts, entertainments, all sorts of things. I don't know how I'm going to manage them all. Here's this big Police Concert, one of the first. A policeman brought tickets for it to the door yesterday - such a big, fine-looking fellow - with a revolver. I took two tickets. My, that will be a great evening, all those policemen singing together. But I don't know whether I'll go. Such a lot of police, eh?... But I've got the tickets up on the mantel alongside of the Firemen's Entertainment, and the Musicale for the Deaf and Dumb, and a lot more. That one on the right is a new one - the Garbage Men's Gathering. I got that from the garbage man early this morning. My goodness! It was a piece of luck. He told me he had rung the bell twice and was just going away when I came down in my dressing-gown. Wasn't it a lucky chance! And, do you know, he says it's a new thing this Christmas, the first time the garbage men have got together. Think of it - ever since the birth of Christ.

But the bother is it's the same night as the Archaeology lecture at the university and I musn't miss that. Mrs. Dim - she's the wife of Professor Dim who's giving the lecture - sent me a ticket. I had sent her an azalea and she sent back the ticket right away - pretty thoughtful, eh? - and afterwards I met her on the street and she said I really must come. She said this is his new lecture. He's only been giving it since 1935. So there's the ticket on the mantelpiece. The Record of the Rocks, it reads - Great title, eh? you'd wonder how a man could get a title like that. Mrs. Dim told me that Professor Dim thought and thought and thought, before he got it. I'll say he did, eh?

But of course there's one thing I certainly won't miss, and that's church on Sunday morning. I'm not much of a church-goer as a rule, but I never miss Christmas morning. Canon Bleet always preaches himself. He's past eighty now, but my! he's a vigorous old man! He preached an hour and a quarter last Christmas - and such a sermon. He just took the text, "Come!" - just that one word, "Come" - or, no, wait a minute, it was "Up!"... It was about the Hittites. He went back to Genesis, then right down to the apostles and half way back again. So I'm not going to miss that. I don't know what it's going to be this year. I hope it'll be the Hittites again, eh?

So when you put it all together, it begins to look like a pretty big day, doesn't it? And naturally the biggest part of it is Christmas Dinner! Such a dinner as I had last year at the Dobson-Dudds, a real, old-fashioned dinner, right after Church. Eat! I never ate so much in my life - turkey, plum pudding, everything. You see what makes you eat at their house is they don't have anything to drink. They are against it. Dudd told me so himself, right after we got into the house, after I'd taken my coat off. He said they're

14

against it, on principle. Mrs. Dudd said so too, in the drawing-room. They have a lovely place, perfectly beautiful, and so hospitable! Mrs. Dudd says she calls it Liberty Hall, because she lets people do just as they like. But, as she said, she's against having anything to drink because of the children seeing it. You see, Mrs. Dudd was a Dobson, and all the Dobsons were against it. Old Mrs. Dobson - Mrs. Dudd's mother - was there at the dinner - that was good, wasn't it? - She sat next to me, and she told me they had always been against it. She told me she didn't know where the young people were getting to now; she said you go to dinner where the young girls drink cock-tails and wine till it's just awful! Say - think if I'd got into a dinner like that!

But, of course, there's one good thing about not having to drink, you certainly can eat. I mean, not only turkey and that, but a lot of extra things. I ate celery all the time I was waiting for the turkey. You naturally do if there's no sherry. I ate bunches of it, and afterwards a lot of parsley and part of a table wreath by mistake.

Such a dinner! We went into the drawing-room afterwards and it was great. We didn't smoke because Mrs. Dudd doesn't believe in gentlemen smoking when ladies are present. She thinks that the ladies' company ought to be enough without. So it ought, oughtn't it? However, we had a fine time looking at the photographs taken of their summer place - Liberty Cottage. I had to leave about five o'clock for Canon Dim's Happy Sunday Afternoon (he has it on Christmas, too) for the News Boys. I just made it.

Of course, naturally the great excitement before Christmas time is the question of buying presents. It takes a tremendous lot of thinking about because the real thing in giving is to think just what people would like and what would be suitable and acceptable - the kind of thing a person would like to have and keep. Often it's puzzling to know what to give. Now there's Horton. He's a stockbroker downtown, and I see him often at the club, and I must give him something this year because he sent me an azalea. It was the one I sent to Mrs. Dim. Horton has a client who is a florist, and of course that started it. Now you see, I have to give a present to Horton - he's the one I say is a broker - I can't really tell what I ought to give, as it all de-pends on the market. I had thought of giving him a Turkish rose-water Narghile pipe - but if the market all goes bad again, it might be a winter overcoat.

I said I had "thought of giving - " That's the thing, "thinking of something to give," even if in the end you don't feel quite sure and don't give it. For example, I am giving Canon Bleet an encyclopaedia. Isn't that just exactly, absolutely the thing for a scholarly clergyman? Can't you just see him starting right in at Capital A. and reading it all! But wait, he mustn't have it yet! You see encyclopaedias get so quickly out of date. Wait! - patience! - till the very year when there's a new one, for example, the last edition of Britannica came out in 1927. Canon Bleet knows all that happened up to then. So I've been waiting each year to hit it right. So far no luck. But I happen to know, on the inside, that there's to be a new edition any time within ten years. That's the one for him, eh?

On the other hand, some presents - I've got. I have them right here in the room - things that I wanted to make sure of. This dressing gown (the one I have on) is for my brother George. When I got it, a little while ago, it looked a little bit too new, so I've been taking the edge off it, and of course I can't have any buttons sewn on or the ink taken out. Then here's this present for Teddy. Teddy travels a good deal, so guess what I've got him! - a travelling bag! Pretty good idea, eh? - the kind of bag you take when you travel. It's made of pigskin. The man said so, but to look at a pig you wouldn't think it. It's too clean for a pig. I've taken a trip or two with it just to get it more like the natural pig before Teddy gets it.

And yet, somehow, I now and then think that perhaps this Christmas I'll break away a little. After all, a man ought not to get into a rut. So much church-going (every year) is apt to get a man stuck in a groove.

And the Christmas dinner stuff! The Dobson-Dudds have invited me to come again for Christmas dinner this year. But I don't think I can go. Oh, no, I mustn't. It would be imposing on them. A man mustn't always be taking the hospitality of his friends. I think this year I'll just go down and have a bite to eat at the club, with just a glass of sherry and just a bottle of red wine or a quart of Scotch whiskey. Just that.

No, I'm not sure I won't alter it at all. It's too exciting, too wearing - concerts, sermons, I can't keep up with it. Perhaps I'll pack up George's dressing gown into Teddy's pigskin travelling bag and beat it out of town. Where? I don't know - perhaps I'll go up north? eh, or down south? or, say - out west, or perhaps back east, anyway, somewhere!

MERRY CHRISTMAS

"**M**y Dear Young Friend," said Father Time, as he laid his hand gently upon my shoulder, "you are entirely wrong."

Then I looked up over my shoulder from the table at which I was sitting and I saw him.

But I had known, or felt, for at least the last half-hour that he was standing somewhere near me.

You have had, I do not doubt, good reader, more than once that strange uncanny feeling that there is someone unseen standing beside you, in a darkened room, let us say, with a dying fire, when the night has grown late, and the October wind sounds low outside, and when, through the thin curtain that we call Reality, the Unseen World starts for a moment clear upon our dreaming sense.

You have had it? Yes, I know you have. Never mind telling me about it. Stop. I don't want to hear about that strange presentiment you had the night your Aunt Eliza broke her leg. Don't let's bother with your experience. I want to tell mine.

"You are quite mistaken, my dear young friend," repeated Father Time, "quite wrong."

"Young friend?" I said, my mind, as one's mind is apt to in such a case, running to an unimportant detail. "Why do you call me young?"

"Your pardon," he answered gently - he had a gentle way with him, had Father Time. "The fault is in my failing eyes. I took you at first sight for something under a hundred."

"Under a hundred?" I expostulated. "Well, I should think so!"

"Your pardon again," said Time, "the fault is in my failing memory. I forgot. You seldom pass that nowadays, do you? Your life is very short of late."

I heard him breathe a wistful hollow sigh. Very ancient and dim he seemed as he stood beside me. But I did not turn to look upon him. I had no need to. I knew his form, in the inner and clearer sight of things, as well as every human being knows by innate instinct, the Unseen face and form of Father Time.

I could hear him murmuring beside me, "Short - short, your life is short;" till the sound of it seemed to mingle with the measured ticking of a clock somewhere in the silent house.

Then I remembered what he had said.

"How do you know that I am wrong?" I asked. "And how can you tell what I was thinking?"

"You said it out loud," answered Father Time. "But it wouldn't have mattered, anyway. You said that Christmas was all played out and done with."

"Yes," I admitted, "that's what I said."

"And what makes you think that?" he questioned, stooping, so it seemed to me, still further over my shoulder.

"Why," I answered, "the trouble is this. I've been sitting here for hours, sitting till goodness only knows how far into the night, trying to think out something to write for a Christmas story. And it won't go. It can't be done - not in these awful days."

"A Christmas Story?"

"Yes. You see, Father Time," I explained, glad with a foolish little vanity of my trade to be able to tell him something that I thought enlightening, "all the Christmas stuff - stories and jokes and pictures - is all done, you know, in October."

I thought it would have surprised him, but I was mistaken.

"Dear me," he said, "not till October! What a rush! How well I remember in Ancient Egypt - as I think you call it - seeing them getting out their Christmas things, all cut in hieroglyphics, always two or three years ahead."

"Two or three years!" I exclaimed.

"Pooh," said Time, "that was nothing. Why in Babylon they used to get their Christmas jokes ready - all baked in clay - a whole Solar eclipse ahead of Christmas. They said, I think, that the public preferred them so."

"Egypt?" I said. "Babylon? But surely, Father Time, there was no Christmas in those days. I thought - "

"My dear boy," he interrupted gravely, "don't you know that there has always been Christmas?"

I was silent. Father Time has moved across the room and stood beside the fireplace, leaning on the mantlepiece. The little wreaths of smoke from the fading fire seemed to mingle with his shadowy outline.

"Well," he said presently, "what is it that is wrong with Christmas?"

"Why," I answered, "all the romance, the joy, the beauty of it has gone, crushed and killed by the greed of commerce and the horrors of war. I am not, as you thought I was, a hundred years old, but I can conjure up, as anybody can, a picture of Christmas in the good old days of a hundred years ago: the quaint old-fashioned houses, standing deep among the evergreens, with the light twinkling from the windows on the snow; the warmth and comfort within; the great fire roaring on the hearth; the merry guests grouped about its blaze and the little children with their eyes dancing in the Christmas firelight, waiting for Father Christmas in his fine mummery of red and white and cotton wool to hand the presents from the yuletide tree. I can see it," I added, "as if it were yesterday."

"It was but yesterday," said Father Time, and his voice seemed to soften with the memory of bygone years. "I remember it well."

"Ah," I continued, "that was Christmas indeed. Give me back such days as those, with the old good cheer, the old stagecoaches and the gabled inns and the warm red wine, the snapdragon and the Christmas-tree, and I'll believe again in Christmas, yes, in Father Christmas himself."

"Believe in him?" said Time quietly. "You may well do that. He happens to be standing outside in the street at this moment."

"Outside?" I exclaimed. "Why don't he come in?"

"He's afraid to," said Father Time. "He's frightened and he daren't come in unless you ask him. May I call him in?"

I signified assent, and Father Time went to the window for a moment and beckoned into the darkened street. Then I heard footsteps, clumsy and hesitant they seemed, upon the stairs. And in a moment a figure stood framed in the doorway - the figure of Father Christmas. He stood shuffling his feet, a timid, apologetic look upon his face.

How changed he was!

I had known in my mind's eye, from childhood up, the face and form of Father Christmas as well as that of Old Time himself. Everybody knows, or once knew him - a jolly little rounded man, with a great muffler wound about him, a packet of toys upon his back and with such merry, twinkling eyes and rosy cheeks as are only given by the touch of the driving snow and the rude fun of the North Wind. Why, there was once a time, not yet so long ago, when the very sound of his sleighbells sent the blood running warm to the heart.

But now how changed.

All draggled with the mud and rain he stood, as if no house had sheltered him these three years past. His old red jersey was tattered in a dozen places, his muffler frayed and ravelled.

The bundle of toys that he dragged with him in a net, seemed wet and worn till the cardboard boxes gaped asunder. There were boxes among them, I vow, that he must have been carrying these three past years.

But most of all I noted the change that had come over the face of Father Christmas. The old brave look of cheery confidence was gone. The smile that had beamed responsive to the laughing eyes of countless children around unnumbered Christmas-trees was there no more. And in the place of it there showed a look of timid apology, of apprehensiveness, as of one who has asked in vain the warmth and shelter of a human home - such a look as the harsh cruelty of this world has stamped upon the face of its outcasts.

So stood Father Christmas shuffling upon the threshold, fumbling his poor tattered hat in his hand.

"Shall I come in?" he said, his eyes appealingly on Father Time.

"Come," said Time. He turned to speak to me, "Your room is dark. Turn up the lights. He's used to light, bright light and plenty of it. The dark has frightened him these three years past."

I turned up the lights and the bright glare revealed all the more cruelly the tattered figure before us.

Father Christmas advanced a timid step across the floor. Then he paused, as if in sudden fear!

"Is this floor mined?" he said.

"No, no." said Time soothingly. And to me he added in a murmured whisper, "He's afraid. He was blown up in a mine in No Man's Land between the trenches at Christmas-time in 1914. It broke his nerve."

"May I put my toys on that machine gun?" asked Father Christmas timidly. "It will help to keep them dry."

"It is not a machine gun," said Time gently. "See, it is only a pile of books upon the sofa." And to me he whispered, "They turned a machine gun on him in the streets of Warsaw. He thinks he sees them everywhere since then."

"It's all right, Father Christmas," I said, speaking as cheerily as I could, while I rose and stirred the fire into a blaze. "There are no machine guns here and there are no mines. This is but the house of a poor writer."

"Ah," said Father Christmas, lowering his tattered hat still further and attempting something of a humble bow, "a writer? Are you Hans Andersen, perhaps?"

"Not quite," I answered.

"But a great writer, I do not doubt," said the old man, with a humble courtesy that he had learned, it well may be, centuries ago in the yuletide season of his northern home. "The world owes much to its great books. I carry some of the greatest with me always. I have them here - "

He began fumbling among the limp and tattered packages that he carried. "Look! The House that Jack Built - a marvellous, deep thing, sir - and this, The Babes in the Wood. Will you take it, sir? A poor present, but a present still - not so long ago I gave them in thousands every Christmas-time. None seem to want them now."

He looked appealingly towards Father Time, as the weak may look towards the strong, for help and guidance.

"None want them now," he repeated, and I could see the tears start in his eyes. "Why is it so? Has the world forgotten its sympathy with the lost children wandering in the wood?"

"All the world," I heard Time murmur with a sigh, "is wandering in the wood." But out loud he spoke to Father Christmas in cheery admonition, "Tut, tut, good Christmas," he said, "you must cheer up. Here, sit in this chair the biggest one; so - beside the fire. Let us stir it to a blaze; more wood, that's better. And listen, good old Friend, to the wind outside - almost a Christmas wind, is it not? Merry and boisterous enough, for all the evil times it stirs among."

Old Christmas seated himself beside the fire, his hands outstretched towards the flames. Something of his old-time cheeriness seemed to flicker across his features as he warmed himself at the blaze.

"That's better," he murmured. "I was cold, sir, cold, chilled to the bone. Of old I never felt it so; no matter what the wind, the world seemed warm about me. Why is it not so now?"

"You see," said Time, speaking low in a whisper for my ear alone, "how sunk and broken he is? Will you not help?"

"Gladly," I answered, "if I can."

"All can," said Father Time, "every one of us."

Meantime Christmas had turned towards me a questioning eye, in which, however, there seemed to revive some little gleam of merriment.

"Have you, perhaps," he asked half timidly, "schnapps?"

"Schnapps?" I repeated.

"Ay, schnapps. A glass of it to drink your health might warm my heart again, I think."

"Ah," I said, "something to drink?"

"His one failing," whispered Time, "if it is one. Forgive it him. He was used to it for centuries. Give it him if you have it."

"I keep a little in the house," I said reluctantly perhaps, "in case of illness."

"Tut, tut," said Father Time, as something as near as could be to a smile passed over his shadowy face. "In case of illness! They used to say that in ancient Babylon. Here, let me pour it for him. Drink, Father Christmas, drink!"

Marvellous it was to see the old man smack his lips as he drank his glass of liquor neat after the fashion of old Norway.

Marvellous, too, to see the way in which, with the warmth of the fire and the generous glow of the spirits, his face changed and brightened till the old-time cheerfulness beamed again upon it.

He looked about him, as it were, with a new and growing interest.

"A pleasant room," he said. "And what better, sir, than the wind without and a brave fire within!"

Then his eye fell upon the mantelpiece, where lay among the litter of books and pipes a little toy horse.

"Ah," said Father Christmas almost gayly, "children in the house!"

"One," I answered, "the sweetest boy in the world."

"I'll be bound he is!" said Father Christmas and he broke now into a merry laugh that did one's heart good to hear.

"They all are! Lord bless me! The number that I have seen, and each and every one - and quite right too - the sweetest child in all the world. And how old, do you say? Two and a half all but two months except a week? The very sweetest age of all, I'll bet you say, eh, what? They all do!"

And the old man broke again into such a jolly chuckling of laughter that his snow-white locks shook upon his head.

"But stop a bit," he added. "This horse is broken. Tut, tut, a hind leg nearly off. This won't do!"

He had the toy in his lap in a moment, mending it. It was wonderful to see, for all his age, how deft his fingers were.

"Time," he said, and it was amusing to note that his voice had assumed almost an authoritative tone, "reach me that piece of string. That's right. Here, hold your finger across the knot. There! Now, then, a bit of beeswax. What? No beeswax? Tut, tut, how ill-supplied your houses are today. How can you mend toys, sir, without beeswax? Still, it will stand up now."

I tried to murmur my best thanks.

But Father Christmas waved my gratitude aside.

"Nonsense," he said, "that's nothing. That's my life. Perhaps the little boy would like a book too. I have them here in the packet. Here, sir, Jack and the Bean Stalk, most profound thing. I read it to myself often still. How damp it is! Pray, sir, will you let me dry my books before your fire?"

"Only too willingly," I said. "How wet and torn they are!"

Father Christmas has risen from his chair and was fumbling among his tattered packages, taking from them his children's books, all limp and draggled from the rain and wind.

"All wet and torn!" he murmured, and his voice sank again into sadness. "I have carried them these three years past. Look! These were for little children in Belgium and in Serbia. Can I get them to them, think you?"

Time gently shook his head.

"But presently, perhaps," said Father Christmas, "if I dry and mend them. Look, some of them were inscribed already! This one, see you, was written 'With father's love!' Why has it never come to him? Is it rain or tears upon the page?"

He stood bowed over his little books, his hands trembling as he turned the pages. Then he looked up, the old fear upon his face again.

"That sound!" he said. "Listen! It is guns - I hear them."

"No, no, I said, "it is nothing. Only a car passing in the street below."

"Listen," he said. "Hear that again - voices crying!"

"No, no," I answered, "not voices, only the night wind among the trees."

"My children's voices!" he exclaimed. "I hear them everywhere - they come to me in every wind - and I see them as I wander in the night and storm - my children - torn and dying in the trenches - beaten into the ground - I hear them crying from the hospitals - each one to me, still as I knew him once, a little child. Time, Time," he cried, reaching out his arms in appeal, "give me back my children!"

"They do not die in vain," Time murmured gently.

But Christmas only moaned in answer:

"Give me back my children!

Then he sank down upon his pile of books and toys, his head buried in his arms.

"You see," said Time, "his heart is breaking, and will you not help him if you can?"

"Only too gladly," I replied. "But what is there to do?"

"This," said Father Time, "listen."

He stood before me grave and solemn, a shadowy figure but half seen though he was close beside me. The firelight had died down, and through the curtained windows there came already the first dim brightening of dawn.

"The world that once you knew," said Father Time, "seems broken and destroyed about you. You must not let them know - the children. The cruelty and the horror and the hate that racks the world today - keep it from them. Some day he will know" - "that his children, that once were, have not died in vain: that from their sacrifice shall come a nobler, better world for all to live in, a world where countless happy children shall hold bright their memory forever. But for the children of Today, save and spare them all you can from the evil hate and horror of the war. Later they will know and understand. Not yet. Give them back their Merry Christmas and its kind thoughts, and its Christmas charity, till later on there shall be with it again Peace upon Earth Good Will towards Men."

His voice ceased. It seemed to vanish, as it were, in the sighing of the wind.

I looked up. Father Time and Christmas had vanished from the room. The fire was low and the day was breaking visibly outside.

"Let us begin," I murmured. "I will mend this broken horse."

LET US BE THANKFUL

A FEW THOUGHTS FOR CHRISTMAS

With the approach of the glad season the thoughts of all pious persons, such as the readers of Vanity Fair, might be turned to the consideration of what a lot we have to be thankful for. Of late there has been a tendency to repine. Again and again I go into a man's office and find him all humped up in his chair repining. I have to lift him up by the coat collar and sit him straight again. After all, whatever troubles there may be around us, here we are on the good old earth still spinning round as usual. When I say *spinning* perhaps I ought to qualify it a little. It appears from the discoveries of Professor Einstein of Berlin made public since last Christmas that she is not spinning quite as she did. It seems that the spacial content of the cone described by the prolongation of the earth's axis is not what we thought it was. But personally I never expected that it would be. Things never are. It is proved now that space is only a relative conception and that the earth is really moving constantly round a corner. This means that the future life of our planet is greatly shorter than had been supposed. Instead of the fifty million years that we had confidently expected, it appears that we are not likely to have more than five million. But what of that? Let us enjoy our five million years while we can. If the earth doesn't spin as well as it did, still it spins. That's something.

Then in the next place we look about us at this glad Yuletide and we see the beautiful prospect of a world at peace. After the long years of war that alone should make us thankful, the mere thought that at last we have peace. At least, when one says *peace*, I suppose more properly one ought to modify the expression just a little bit. From last week's paper it seems that the Bolsheviki, about a million of them, took a drive at the Ukranians and that the little Russians, about ten hundred thousand of the wee fellows, are getting ready for a drive against the Letts and the Liths. But let them drive. They've got the driving habit. And anyway I don't believe they really hurt one another. So, too, the Hindoos are in a state of effervescence. All right, let them seethe. I understand that at any moment a republican revolution may break out. Italy and a monarchical counter revolution may overwhelm Germany. The Arabs in Africa are talking about a *Jehab* or sacred war against the Christians, and the Christians are plotting against the French. On our own side of the water they say the ground beneath our feet is honeycombed with radical insurrection. Mexico is said to be preparing to invade the United States and the Virgin Islands are on the brink of a declaration of independence.

Still all said and done this is peace. Let us look abroad and enjoy the prospect. It seems almost too bright to last. But at least if anyone breaks it we can write and tell the League of Nations on them.

One turns to the home. Is it not at least something to be thankful for at Christmas time that we still have a roof above our heads to shelter us? When I say 'we have a roof', possibly I would be better to shade the expression somewhat. It is unfortunately true that a good many of us have no roof owing to the shortage of houses. The census now shows about 105,000,000 people in the United States with only housing accommodation for 100,000,000. There are 5,000,000 homeless people among us this Christmas time. It is only too true. I have myself seen them sitting round in the cabarets and palm rooms at two o'clock in the morning.

Another very real reason that we have for being thankful is at last the dreadful pressure of the high cost of living is passing away. Prices are coming down. Wheat fell two cents last week. Rolled iron is at least two dollars a ton and steel in bars is getting cheaper every day. In other words all the old home comforts are coming back to us. Crude oil came down four cents yesterday and oats went down eight cents a bushel. Any man can step out this Christmas Eve to fetch home a gallon of crude oil and a peck of oats and put six cents clear profit into his pocket. More than this, the market reports show that leather is very restless, the pulp is nervous, and that there is strong undercurrent in cement, and an absolute collapse of bricks and tiles. I tell you, we are coming in our own very fast.

Another cause that I find for devout gratitude, at this season of the year, lies in the improved way in which of late we have learned to keep Christmas Day. We are at least getting our Christmas Day functions on a proper professional basis, in keeping with the spirit of the time. In the church, which I don't attend, the Christmas morning service used to be disfigured by the singing of such things as "Hark the Herald Angels Sing" by the entire congregation in unison. As I remember, we used to stand up and sing it all together. The discordance was such that one could hardly hear oneself sing. We have now changed all that. This Christmas we have enjoyed a professional quartette, four of the very biggest people on the Vaudeville Circuit. We are to pay them a hundred dollars each with a percentage in the offertory. They are to sing us an anthem, an aria that we engaged a man, one of the principal librettists of the New York stage to write for us. The anthem is to consist simply of the word *Hark*! repeated in various ways. We, the congregation (I say "we" for I have invited a party of friends to come with me after a breakfast at one of the hotels) are simply to sit in our places and the quartet will sing *Hark* till the pastor pushes a button for them to stop. We don't have to pray at all, or to move. If the applause warrants it there is to be, as an encore, a solo anthem by the tenor. He is to sing "Now a Heavenly Child is Born" but he is not to use it all but just to take the word *Now* and keep singing it. If he is not called for, we pay him nothing. After the singing in place of the old fashioned sermon that used to be so wearisome we are to have a set of moving pictures. It is a reel that we had made specially. It shows ourselves, the congregation. First we are standing outside the church talking, and then it shows us going into the church talking and then coming out talking on the steps. It is wonderfully interesting and we think it will put a lot of 'pep' into the service and be a big add. Then to keep the religious tone of it up we have inserted titles run through the film that read "Christmas! Christmas! who was born on Christmas, Rah! Rah! Rah!

I have no doubt that a great many other churches are planning a Christmas service of this kind or something close to it. But the church service is only a part of the new Christmas. Among other changes that we've been making lately is that we've quite done away with the old fashioned family dinner with the children lined up on each side of the table and with grace at the beginning and crackers at the end. Now we eat our Christmas dinner at a hotel. There is no doubt there's a touch about a hotel that you can never get at home. After all at home if you say Grace, who hears it? On the other hand if at a hotel, without in the least posing about it, you rise reverently and ask God to bless the food, you feel that at least someone is listening to you. Then at a hotel it is so pleasant on Christmas Day to feel one's self among strangers. I don't mean to say that one's friends are not all right, but when you want a really good time, at which you feel that you are taken at your full worth it so much more delightful to be among strangers. They are so responsive. They laugh so easily at the lightest joke that it's a pleasure to be among them.

And what's more, if I want to pull one end of a Christmas cracker, I don't want a child at the other end of it. A child isn't strong enough. It is much wiser to have nice strong women, not too old or she might be weak, and preferably in evening dress so that the cracker won't burn her.

After all, it is not such a sad world as you might think. Is it?

FIRST AID TO THE CHRISTMAS TOURIST

AN ATTEMPT TO LIGHTEN HIS BURDEN OF INFORMATION

It has often occurred to me that in the current travellers' guide books, advertisements and travel 'literature', a great wrong is being done to the unfortunate tourists. The writers of these little books and phamphlets seem to be labouring under a misapprehension. They take for granted that a tourist is a man, crazy over history, with a perfect thirst for dates, for memorials and survivals and the past. They presume that if there is anything in the way of a tombstone within ten miles he will be wild to see it. And that if you can show him a rock on which Charlemagne once sat, he takes a twenty-four hour round trip just to sit on it.

When the tourist is not busy with history, tombstones and graveyards, he is supposed to get excited over folklore, old customs and the dress of the peasants. When this flags, the tourist is expected to fall back on geological information, altitude above the sea, and relative rainfall.

Thus, his pretty little vacation is filled up with examining what the peasants wear, how high they are above the sea, how much rain falls on them each year, and whose grave is said by tradition to be situated at, or near, their village.

Now, as a matter of fact, this kind of tourist lived in the days of Washington Irving, a hundred years before Sunday afternoon information on the radio, and is as dead as Washington Irving is.

Let me illustrate, and help to amend the situation by taking as a case in point, my own good old province of Quebec, already buried under its December snow and ready for the advent of the Christmas tourist from New

York. This year, when he comes, let there be no misunderstanding. Let us see just where the guide books will need a little correction.

"It is not without a thrill of romantic interest," so the guide book opens up, "that we find ourselves on our journey northward from New York, swiftly borne along in the night through the great forests of the Adirondacks and thundering through the darkness along the historic shores of Lake Champlain. The broad surface of the lake lies sleeping under its winter mantle of snow."

Quite so, and so we don't see it; the lake is frozen, and it's night and it's dark and we're asleep and we don't see it. We didn't come to see it, either. No passengers, except crooks, stay awake in an Adirondack sleeper at three o'clock in the morning. So much for Lake Champlain.

"We are now," so rattles on the guide book, "in a country replete with historic interest. It was here that the heroic Montcalm stormed Fort Ticonderoga, here that Ethan Allan overwhelmed the slumbering British; here General Burgoyne, hopelessly surrounded, made his last stand on Bunker's Hill while Sitting Bull and his mounted braves closed in upon his devoted band with Sheridan still forty miles away" exactly so. But we learned all that stuff in Grade Ten of our High School Course and we passed our examination and are done with it. Anyway we're still asleep.

So the guide book has to strike a new note. "We have now passed the height of land and are speeding down the Appalachian slope into the Laurentian plain. The rugged massif of the Adirondack is exchanged for the broad valley of the Richelieu, an alluvial plain thrown up, perhaps, in the post-prandial epoch. The soil about is a congolomerate semi-introgenous loam; our altitude is now 200 feet with a saturation of 75 per cent and a barometric air pressure of twenty seven decimal three."

Precisely. But as a matter of fact we are in the dressing room of the car trying to shave and we do not propose to risk cutting our throats in the interests of geological science.

So the guide book goes off on another attack and takes up its favourite lines of manner, customs and the peasantry. This sort of thing worked for so many centuries in Europe, that it is hard to let it go.

"We are now," says the enthusiastic announcement, "passing through some of the oldest settlements of *La Nouvelle France.* We observe the quaint houses, taken as it was straight out of old Normandy, with the solid stone walls, the high gabled roofs and the little windows of the *dortoir* projecting high above the *fenetres* of the *cuisine*. Behind is the *écurie* of the cows nestled beside its pleasant *fumier*."

That's enough of the French. Will the guide book people never understand that we speak nothing but our own language, acquired at great difficulty and cost and already brought as near to perfection as we hope to go. This is all that we can afford.

But we know of course, what the next item will be, the 'picturesque peasant'. All right. Bring him on "As we pass the quaint farmsteads half buried in the snow, we note here and there the characteristic figure of a *habitant*, half buried in the snow, seated in his one horse sleigh or *calèche*, his rough country horse or *cheval*, half buried."

That's all right, bury him and be done with it. It is strange that the guide books are unable to learn that human beings now-a-days are all alike everywhere. A Chinaman from Shanghai and a Pygmy from Equatorial Africa and a high school teacher from Oklahoma, are all the same. They all see the same movies, hear the same radio and all lost money when the stock exchange broke. The picturesque differences are all gone. Turks wear American shoes, Americans wear Hindu pyjamas, Hindus wear English shirts and English students wear Turkish trousers. The picturesque peasant belongs back in the days of Voltaire. Today, when the Eskimo smokes cigars in his igloo and the Patagonian football team plays home-and-home games with the French penal settlement at Devil's Island, what's the good of pretending any more.

But at last, after passing through all the scenery and history and geology and local colour, the guide book finds itself arriving at last at a real city, let us say, the city of Montreal. Here at last is something lifelike and animation, taxicabs, noise, restaurants beefsteak, life. But can the guide book see it? No.

As we disentrain ourselves at Montreal we realize that we are at the very spot where the intrepid Jacques Cartier stood in amazement within the great stockaded port of Hochelaga (1535) or where the gallant company of the Sieur de Maisonneuve prepared in 1645, the fortified towns beside the great river which was to witness the surrender of Vaudreuil to General Amherst in 1760 which prepared the way for its capture in 1775 by the American General Montgomery, who little thought that the same scene would witness the building of the Grand Trunk Railway in 1856 which culminated in the world war of 1914.

After which having insinuated the history of the city in this painless fashion into the visitor, the guide book goes on to give him the really up-to-date information about the city of today. Thus: "The chief points of interest in the present city are the site of old Hochelaga (exact position unknown), the grave of the Sieur de Maisonneuve (the location of which is disputed) and the burial places of Hiawatha, Pocahontas and other early pioneers."

I suppose there must be people to whom this kind of information is welcome, and this aspect of travel congenial. There *must* be, otherwise the little guide books and the illustrated travel booklets would cease to live. Presumably there are people who come home from their vacation tours and carry on conversations, something like this: -

"You were in Montreal on your vacation, were you not?"

"Yes, the city was founded by Maisonneuve in 1645."

"Was it indeed! And what is it's altitude above the sea?"

"It's mean altitude above high tide is 40 feet but the ground on which the city stands rises to a magnificent elevation, or mountain, which attains a height of 600 feet."

"Does it indeed, and has this elevation a name?"

"It has. It is known as Mount Royal, a name conferred upon it by its first discoverer, Jacques or Jim Cartier."

"Really, and what is the annual rainfall?"

"Well, the annual rainfall, if you include the precipitation of snow" -

"Oh yes, I do, of course."

"In that case, it would be about fifty inches."

"Indeed! What a fascinating vacation you must have had."

"We did, I recall one very odd old habitant, or peasant" -

"Do you, but, if you don't mind, just recall him to yourself, I fear I absolutely have to go."

Instead of the mournful and misleading information about history and the peasantry, how much better if the guide book would drop on the side, a few little items of real and useful information, as -

"The exact site of the old French town may be said to be in a straight line between the Molson's Brewery (now running) and the Dow's Brewery (still brewing). The house occupied by General Montgomery in 1775 is easily found by its proximity to the principal offices of the Quebec Legion Commission."

That would be something, indeed. But I suppose that in this peculiar world all of us, tourists and all, love a little pretense and magniloquence. We like to pretend that we travel for the sake of history and archeology, that we want dates, facts, ruins, chronology and tombstones.

The open and brutal confession that holidays are for enjoyment would seem too crude.

Never mind. Get into a comfortable train and come along and visit dear Old Quebec Province buried under her mantle of snow. Don't stay awake at night: never mind the peasantry: forget Maisonneauve and General Montgomery. Just have a good time.

MERRY CHRISTMAS, MARS

AN OPTIMIST SENDS GREETINGS ACROSS SPACE

Is there people upon Mars?

Well, it certainly seems wonderful to be able to communicate with you people up there! It is only a few weeks ago since they invested at Schenectady this new "light beam method" of sending words along a streak of light and here we are already able to talk across forty million miles of space. Even at that, some of the professors themselves were doubtful about it at first. They said that you people might not have any receivers, or that the message might get mixed up and come out all backwards. But that's all right, you boys will pick it up right enough.

So it gives me a chance to hand out to you the first information about this world of ours that you have ever had. There seems so much to say that it's hard to know where to begin. I know some of you will want me to start right off on prohibition, or women, or sport, or perhaps on war reparations and war debts and whether your depression will end before ours.

But I'll just have to begin in the best way I can.

Well, to start on, we've just had a big election down here, and of course that's always the biggest piece of good-natured fun in our lives. Mr. Hoover, - you've heard of him - was pretending to run against Mr. Roosevelt and Mr. Roosevelt was making out, in a good natured way, that he was running against Mr. Hoover. So it made no end of good feeling. Even now after it's over, Mr. Hoover likes to pretend that Mr. Roosevelt is President and Mr. Roosevelt likes to pretend that Mr. Hoover is. So you see, for each thing that comes up Mr. Hoover says "You do it" and Mr. Roosevelt says "No, no, you do it". So, of course, that makes quite a laugh. For instance, there is this question of giving the English 95,000,000 dollars of which you've heard something. Mr. Hoover wants Mr. Roosevelt to give it to them but he says, "No, you give it". And that makes lots of fun. Of course, the English don't want it, or at least, they think it would be nicer for us if they took it now and then later, say a hundred years later, gave it back again - or say two hundred years later.

But the English money wasn't the only item of fun we had round election time. We had perhaps even more over the question of being 'wet' or 'dry'. I imagine, from what they tell me of your planet that you have that something too. Part of the time your country is all dried up and the moisture all collects in a big polar ice-cap and presently comes running down in a perfect flood all over everywhere. Well, it's like that with us too. Part of the time we get dry, and then the moisture all collects up north (we call our ice-cap Canada) and then down it comes again. It's coming now. So that makes for a lot of amusement and fooling and good feeling. It means that we shall have to start and make great quantities of beer, and some of the people are afraid that we can't drink it. Others say, it's all right, leave it to them. They don't need help.

In fact, it's not so much a question of making the beer, as how to serve it out. Everybody seems agreed that we don't want the old saloon again, you've heard of the old saloon with the bar all along one side? - well, nobody wants the saloon back. The service was too slow. Often you'd have to stand in line for four or five minutes waiting before you got anything. What is needed is something quicker. They have a fine scheme up in Canada called Liquor Control whereby everybody has to buy at least twenty-six drinks of whiskey at a time. We may use that or something quicker still. At any rate, there would be lots of good natured chaff and banter on the subject when the congress gets laughing over it.

But I was talking a minute ago about England and perhaps you didn't understand that that is a part of Europe. You could pretty well see Europe from Mars even without a glass, I guess. Just by the outline you can see it is all broken up into crooked parts and that means it's all full of nations, and, of course, one of the great things with us now is the big friendliness that has sprung up among all the nations.

In the old days, nations meant war. Now it's just the other way. They've all joined in a big League, with a game about once a week. Last year, China and Japan played off the finals, Japan against China.

All the nations are out now for peace and that makes good feeling everywhere. They all realize that war armament was a terrible burden and they intend to get rid of it. So it has started a sort of contest in generosity as to who will do most. England has offered to pay the whole cost of naval defense, the others need buy no ships at all, but the French say, No, no they'll buy some and the Italians say they'll contribute too, and soon. For a good while the Germans were let off altogether because all the others knew they were hard up, but now the Germans say they can easily afford it and they offer to pay as much or more than anybody. So you can easily imagine what fun and excitement it all is.

One thing that helps to keep up the sport in Europe is the class of men they have over there. There is one fellow called De Valera and I suppose he's about the most comical genius in the world. He lives over in Ireland and, say, the messages he sends over to England would make you die laughing. Then they sauce back at him and keep it going from both sides. Of course, it's only just play, they don't really mean it. De Valera makes out that the Irish won't pay any more rent for Ireland. Well, you know what the Irish are like. What they always like best about having a house is refusing to pay rent on it. In the old days they made a regular game of it and call it "Eviction" and the English would put the Irish out into the snow and they'd all roar with laughter over it. Well, the old system came to an end and the boys in Ireland miss it, so De Valera is daring the English to come over and evict them. Just his fun!

Then there's Germany - you know Germany where the German-Americans came from? and they've got a little fellow there called Hitler - Jimmy Hitler, I think-anyway one of the Hitler boys.

You'd like him if you knew him. He's such a cute little card and always getting up some new piece of fun with the old President Hindenburg. Hindenburg you know is about the biggest man in Europe, but the young fellows like Hitler like to have a little fun with him just the same. The old man is trying to get together a cabinet, and Hitler, just when it's all ready, comes in and puts carpet tacks on the seats or puts pepper on the stove. Then the old man chases them all out. They were let off all together because all the others knew they were hard up, but now the Germans say they can easily afford it and they offer to pay as much or more than anybody. So you can easily imagine what fun and excitement it all is.

Of course it's quieter over on our side of the ocean but still, what with one thing and another, there's a lot of quiet amusement. One great thing just now is there's so much leisure. Ever so many of the boys, millions of them are taking time off, - not working; and anyway there's hardly any work to do. We're getting it down finer and finer all the time. Soon there'll be no work.

The farmers were the ones who started it. You know what they're like, big-hearted fellows, can't bear to ask a man to pay money for anything. So they started giving away wheat, just giving it away (they said so themselves) or if people wouldn't take it like that, asking just a nominal sum like 40 cents a bushel. Corn too and hogs, gave it all away. Last year, just for fun, they threw a whole lot of produce, cart loads of melons or something into the Potomac (you know where that is). Some of them went out and ploughed down whole fields of tomatoes, why? - just playfulness, sheer sense of fun - times so good, such lots of everything. I doubt whether you've ever had such good times up there as we're getting.

So of course as so many of the boys are not working they have time to get up parades and processions and things like that, with music and flags, it's almost as good as war. Often they get up big hikes across country. Once a lot of them walked clear to Washington and when they got there, there was so much fun in the streets, jostling the police and fooling round. They had to ask them to go away.

But all that is really only about one-tenth of the sport we're having. It's not only of the farms, it's in the cities too. There we've got a big joke going round that we call 'deflation of money', a scheme that works out so that every dollar you spend buys twice what it used to. Then you go home and cut your salary in two because you don't need the other half and of course when you all do that it makes everything cheaper still and you have to cut your salary again. It's just a scream who can keep it up longest.

So you see, things are pretty bright down here. What with politics and reparations and deflations and international relations, there's more law and disorder here than we ever enjoyed before. It gets too much for some of the fellows. They take a big laugh and blow their brains out.

But the particular point is that just now it's Christmas time, I suppose you have Christmas up there, and at that time of year we always have an old custom down here of pretending that everything is going fine, even if it isn't. If we can't straighten a thing out, at any rate we have a good laugh over it. I admit that in spite of all I told you above, things look pretty tough on our world just for the present. Europe all tied up, no debts paid, unemployment, bootleggers failing every day, bankers going on the farms, and farmers counting on the banks. If you really started to worry about it, you might get into a bad state. But instead of all that, what we all do down here is to put a little of the real old Christmas spirit with our troubles and chase them away. Go and deflate the grocer for a Christmas turkey, buy a bag full of Christmas presents with a moratorium and have a box of cigars and a fur coat and a gramophone sent up to the house on a hundred year deferred instalment! That's the modus vivendi!

In other words, in spite of all you see and hear up there, our old world is moving still or good-bye. Wave to us when you pass our orbit. Merry Christmas, Mars.

THIS MERRY CHRISTMAS

A CHRISTMAS STAR SHINES THROUGH THE MISTS

This is a Merry Christmas, this Christmas of 1938. I want to say it fairly and decisively and to add that it is on all reasonable grounds the Merriest Christmas that the world has known since the first one. That sounds a big statement, but I can prove it, at least to people with minds as wide as my own. Never, since the Star Risen in the East proclaimed the Christmas from which we date all the others, has there been one that saw the world within nearer reach, within better Hope of that elusive world happiness, forever, always imagined but never achieved - that has been the Allurement and the mainstay of human destiny.

Those who are readers of Charles Dickens will remember a certain character. I think his name was Mr. Montagu Tigg, who was always to be found "round the corner," why he was there, I don't remember, but he seems to be typical of a wider aspect of human kind. It has been the peculiar destiny of man, to be always just about to find happiness, to be always missing it, yet to be on the Hope and 'urge' of it.

Race after race, nation after nation, carries forever the tradition of a coming 'millennium' of a promised land, of a 'Kingdom of Heaven on Earth'. The root idea of it is sunk deep into each of us. Business-men dream of 'good times'; school boys of the Christmas holidays; school girls of ideal husbands. Life lives on expectations. Even the gloomiest Marxian can get fun out of the coming social catastrophe, and the dourest Scot can at least think of damnation. For everybody - something; and for all mankind in the lump, a sort of vast mass yearning, an 'urge', toward a perfected world.

Things that are without this die. The dinosaur of prehistoric times was eighty feet long and could eat a ton of wet grass, without indigestion. Besides man was a puny apelike creature, always puzzled and wishing it could use its thumb. But the dinosaur had no 'pep', no outlook. When the grass got dry it flopped over and died. Man went right on, working on his thumb and urging upward.

This upward urge, so the biologists tell us, is the secret of life itself. This is the 'creative evolution' that fashions all that lives. What makes a certain plant a geranium? Physical and chemical forces that we can estimate itself? Oh, no, the day for such thinking is long gone past. There is something else in it, the thing wants to be geranium. In its dim consciousness, for consciousness reaches down as far as life, and is synonymous with it; it thinks "I mean to be geranium, don't stop me, I've got the geranium idea". And presently it is.

If that is getting too deep into philosophy, come out again. Come back to the undoubted human instinct toward "around the corner happiness," in this hope and expectation of better times just coming. What I am saying here is that at the Christmas close of 1938 and opening of 1939, we are nearer to this unseen goal of peace, plenty and liberty, than ever we were before. If it is still unseen, at least the mist is getting thinner.

I admit that at first sight it doesn't seem so. It also seems a tangle, economics, politics, peace and war, business, trade, all a jumble with nation against nation, class against class, town against town and street against street.

Take our economic life. What a mess. We produce food so easily that we can't eat it; and we can't expect the farmers to eat it themselves. So the price of food falls tells the farmers they can't buy motor cars and the employees in the car business can't buy food. The only thinking then is to destroy the food and scrap the motor cars. That's called the economics of abundance. What is worse, this abundance that starts on the farms sets up an abundance that runs all through industry from trade to trade and back again. If you can't earn wages you can't buy cigars, and if you can't sell cigars you can't buy clothes, and if you can't sell clothes you can't buy boots, and for want of selling boots you can't pay rent for a house and then you are out on the street with no pants and nothing to smoke.

That's the gist of the situation. To say it all out of length in proper economic argument takes two hundred and fifty pages and costs ten fifty.

But as you haven't got ten fifty you can't buy it and had better take it as read.

Now the queerest part of the situation is that if any one of those gears would slip into place, then all the rest would fall into adjustment.

But you see, and now we shift to the larger field of international economics, the moment we try to adjust the gear, in slips the infernal foreigner and upsets everything by offering to trade with it. This low pup offers us food cheaper still, clothes a way less, and boots almost for lacing them up and walking away in them. What can you do? You see this low villain has so depreciated his currency, that is he uses such rotten worthless money, that you daren't trade with him. All you can do is to make your money worse than his, or at least keep edging for worst place (the process called stabilization). Beyond that, the only thing is to stop trade altogether and go in for economic nationalism. When it gets complete the farmer will have to eat his own wheat, the tailor wears his own pants and the bartender drinks his own whiskey.

Even that is not the worst of it, I mean of this apparent appalling outlook for 1938. Economic nationalism breeds political hatred. You can't expect a really high-chested nation to stoop to buy things from other people. They'll sell but they won't buy. They'll borrow but they won't pay. They'll take but they won't give. So the nations fall apart, each thrown on itself, a wolf against the others. Civilization turns to an armed camp, each night is the night before the battle. And not the battle of heroic days, with glittering ranks and high courage and individual valour of which the brave deserve the fair: not that but a hideous conflict of brute slaughter, machinery overwhelming man.

And in all this democracy seems perishing. The liberty and equality of Rousseaus, of Jeffersons, of Cobden and Gladstone, the world of fair plain, equal rights and open speech, all this seems like to smother under a dark rolling cloud of poison gas of [NOT FINISHED]*

All this, I say, seems so. And yet I assert all this is just the dark hour before the dawn. If democracy seems hard put it is because democracy was falling asleep, was forgetting that the price of liberty is eternal vigilance,

---

* The manuscripts for this piece and the one that follows were incomplete. Rather than presume to know the author's precise intention, blanks in the stories were left. Readers are invited to engage in their own imagination. Editor's note.

and that no mere form of government can save if the inner spirit is failing.

Turn again to the items of our seeming world distress that veil for us the Merry Christmas that should be. Here is this uneconomic machine that all clicks wrong, each bit of loosened gear, breaking the connection of the next, till nothing turns and the machine stops. But the *effect* of this is the reverse process must also be true. When one bit begins to click, the next will click and so on all down the line. It's just like what happened in the nursery rhyme about the old woman driving the pig that wouldn't go, who asked the dog to bite the pig to make him go and the dog wouldn't; so she asked the stick (and she did it all in verse, too) to beat the dog, nothing doing, and the fire to burn the stick, and so on all up a chain of effect and cause with the cause not working.

The little nursery audience who waited breathlessly for a cause to break in somewhere and 'start something', little knew that they were getting a firsthand look at what they would someday live to see in the economics of another abundance.

In the old scheme at last something happened. The cat, I think the cat started it, they generally do, began to kill the rat, the rat began to gnaw the rope, the rope began to hang the butcher, the butcher began to kill the ox, the ox began to drink the water, the water began to quench the fire, the fire began to burn the stick, the stick began to beat the dog, the dog began to bite the pig - and THE PIG BEGAN TO GO.

That's the great coming economic event, our pig will begin to go. In response to some unknown economic stimulus - for economics is still an unsolved mystery - our pig will start, and one machine after another, each industry after the next will slide back into gear - revolve and hum. Which is the pig, I don't know. Will it be in 1939? Perhaps, but at any rate we are nearer to it than we ever were before.

One can see even the craziest of our profound remedies, even the wildest of our suggested legislation - if you look at it all together, has got a certain dull luminosity about it, such a powerful light looking through a fog. We propose (some of us) to pension all people over sixty: others, to give two hundred dollars a month to everybody old enough not to save it: others, this is from Alberta and this takes the prize - to pension everybody from birth at the rate of twenty-five dollars a month. All these, and a hundred visionary schemes, as of holidays with pay, of pay without work, are at least the ground swell of an approaching tide. All this is the dawning human consciousness that such a world, - of moderate, of comfortable old age, of money spent? without pinch or afterthought, of youth happy at school, of old age in garrulous ease and even the noon of life carrying its siesta of weekend holiday, that such is possible and some day coming.

The ideas that a hundred years ago would have seemed economic madness - the substitution of idleness for industry, of extravagance for parsimony, of waste for saving, indicate the nebulous material that presently will solidify to a new economic world. And those who have studied the history of the past can judge the hope of the present. Only those who can reconstruct the unutterable poverty of the slums that were, the toil of the factory that was, can see how far even our distracted world has progressed, how full of hope its potential future.

Nor can I believe, and least of all at Christmas time, in the enmity of nations. I think it was Burke - or someone, anyway, who said that he could.

In the old-fashioned way between Kings a fine make-believe was carried on that all the enemy nations were [NOT FINISHED]

Then the war ended, peace was made and the King's sister married the other King's brother, and that made the whole nation loyal friends. The King even broke off a chunk of his subjects and gave them to the King as a mark of esteem.

The shadow of this byegone substance still falls across our world. We do not realize how unified the world is, how much alike we all are, all sitting in at our moving pictures, all playing golf, listening to our radio, copying one another's books and pictures and music. We are on the very edge of world peace and mistake it for world war. Our own power of destruction has filled us with a great obsession of fear. The world is in a nerve crisis, a delirium that calls back for salvation to primitive ideas of conquest, that lost their meaning centuries ago.

This is the situation on which our Christmas star seeks to shine about us. Yet mixed as is the prospect, it contains more real hope in it for peace on earth, good will towards man, than humanity ever saw before.

Now the essence and spirit of Christmas time is this. We first pretend and make-believe that a thing is so, and lo! it presently turns out that it is. We pretend that just for this one day we are the open-hearted, open-handed fellows that our superconsciousness would like us to be - and suddenly we

44

discover that that represents our real selves, not the grouchy, limited, untrusting soul in which we inhabit day by day. Under this Christmas spirit, the dullest dog reaches out for jollity and finds it, the gloomiest man looks out for wit and finds that he has always possessed it; the tightest uncle and the closest godfather opens up their pocket with in sudden generosity, amazed to find that therein lies their real soul. In response to all which the sun shines, the snow sparkles, the plainest girl turns pretty, and the round-est matron drops off twenty years as easily as she dropped her garter twenty years ago, and the little children seen in the light of the candles of the Christmas tree, turn back to angels.

Next day we slump back into usual selves, solemn and tight and appre-hensive. Not for a year can we struggle back again to the Make-Believe world of Christmas, that something tells us is the real one.

Now if we can thus reach out for ultimate truth, at home round a Christmas turkey and a tree, why can't we do that in the big sense, for all the world at a time. Let us but look at the other nations with the Make-Believe of Christmas, and by the same revelation as at home, we shall see them as they really are. The great mass of the people and all the nations are just as we are: the same lives, the same hopes, the same devotions; as willing as we are to be broad and generous and open-handed, if only we dare. Black sheep there are, and always have been, everywhere, and wolves in sheep's clothing. Their power to mislead and to betray ends when the white sheep come together.

Peace on earth, good will towards man, is nearer perhaps this Christ-mas than we know. The mist is clearing from a clouded world and a star rising above it.

CHRISTMAS FICTION AND NATIONAL FRICTION

AN APPLICATION OF THE DEAR OLD CHRISTMAS STORIES TO
NATIONAL HARMONY AND WORLD PEACE

Around the idea of Christmas there has grown up in our fiction a fine literary tradition. Under this convention, Christmas is presumed to be a time of great goodwill, of family reconciliations, a period when old quarrels are forgotten and bygone sins are forgiven. At Christmas time, especially on Christmas Eve when the soft snow is gently falling, the stern old Earl relents, the wayward prodigal comes home, the estranged brothers shake hands, and the banished daughter returns to place the inexplicable infant on its grandfather's knee.

These 'Christmas stories' are familiar to all of us as literature. But no one has yet realized the use that might be made of them in politics. All they need is to be retold in the proper political and international setting, and the good that could be derived from this is incalculable.

Take for example, the well-known Christmas story of the stern old Earl. All his life he has sacrificed affection to rigid principle, sacrificed love to prejudice, and repelled by the unforgiving sterness of his creed, the affection of those whose have been dearest to him. On Christmas Eve, he relents and all is changed. Now observe how this beautiful old story could be revived and applied to the present tariff situation in England, with Lord Snowden cast for the leading part.

I

STORY OF THE REPENTANT EARL

It was Christmas Eve. The stern old Earl sat in his library, his stern old face bent over his desk with its usual stern expression. He was alone in the library. It was late. The fire had burned low.

The stern old Earl wrote on. But as his hand moved over the paper, somehow the sterness seemed to die out of his face, and leave in it nothing but the human kindliness for which nature, long ago had framed it. For he wrote thus: -

"My Dear Stanley

Of late I have been thinking things over and I have come to realize that I have been wrong. I see now that all my ideas about free trade arose only from pride and prejudice. This I must now cast aside. For years I believed, or tried to believe, that industry was limited by the quantity of capital, and that a demand for commodities was not a demand for labour. This led me, as I now freely confess to you, my dear boy, to think that value under free competition was governed by the cost of production, and that unrestricted international trade supplied all consumers with a maximum of goods at a minimum of cost; I see now that this was wrong and wicked, and that while I still have time I must try to set it right, -"

The old Earl paused. He looked up from the paper before him with an expression of firm resolution. For a moment as the eye noted above his desk the portrait of Adam Smith, he seemed to hesitate. Then speaking to himself out loud, he said,

"No, no, I'll do better than write. I'll tell the boy now."

He pulled the bell rope, and to the aged butler who entered he asked: "Can you tell me if Mr. Stanley has gone to bed?"

"I think not, my lord: I think he is still in his sitting room."

"And Master Ramsay and Master Neville?"

"In bed, I think, my lord."

"Very good. Please do not disturb them. But will you ask Mr. Stanley to be kind enough to come down for a moment."

"Grandfather!" exclaimed Stanley as he stepped, with outstretched hands, across the threshold of the library, from which he had been banished for months.

The old Earl clasped the lad to his breast.

"My boy," he said, striving to control the emotion in his voice, "it is Christmas Eve. I have done you a great wrong. I want to try to set it right while I can. I sat down to write to you, but I found it easier and better to speak to you face to face. Stanley, I have been wrong about free trade.."

"Grandfather!"

"Wrong, utterly wrong," continued the old Earl, with something like passion in his voice. "It is not true Stanley, that value under free importation tends to equal the cost of production. I have been wrong, obstinate, pigheaded, but I see it now."

"Not pigheaded, grandfather," exclaimed Stanley, "not pigheaded: a little mulish if you like, but not that. But let me call Ramsay and Neville, do pray."

"No, no," said the Earl, "they are too young to understand."

"Ramsay begins to understand about the tariff, grandfather," said Stanley, "and little Neville seems to have always understood it. I'll call them."

But there was no need. Roused by the unwanted sound of voices in their grandfather's library, little Ramsay and little Neville, still in their sleeping pyjamas, came bursting into the room.

"Ramsay! Neville!" cried Stanley, "isn't it wonderful! Grandfather has given up free trade."

"Grandfather!" exclaimed the little boys.

And at that moment the sound of the church bells, tolling for Christmas Eve, came faintly on the air.

The old Earl moved across the room and drew back the heavy curtain from the French windows. Outside, the bright snow and the air, crystalled with snow flakes, was light with the moonlight.

"Look," he said, "a fall of snow. That will mean a lot of work for the villagers. And work, my children, means wages, for it is true, my dear lads, that a demand for labour is really a demand for commodities."

The old Earl threw open the window.

All four stood listening to the sound of the bells, now loud and clear.

"How beautiful the bells sound!" said little Ramsay.

"Beautiful indeed," said the Earl, "we buy them in Belgium."

"No grandfather," said little Neville gently, "in Birmingham."

II
STORY OF THE CHRISTMAS GHOST

In this story, the most familiar and typical of all, a man, hitherto harsh and remorseless, has a dream of a ghost on Christmas Eve and wakes a changed being. The greatest of all our writers has immortalized the theme as a Christmas tale. But even he never realized the use he might have made of it to settle the most bitter of all political controversies. Here it is retold in its applied form.

Mr. de Valera leaped from his bed in his London lodgings, still filled with the new resolution that had come to him as the result of his dream.

He threw open the window.

Christmas morning! Clear and bright and cold! cold piping for the blood to dance to: "Fine place this town!" thought Mr. de Valera. "Jolly morning for Christmas! Capital to be alive on such a day! Now then, for the new resolutions."

Outside in the street was a boy, swinging on the area railings.

"Hi, you boy!" called Mr. de Valera, "can you tell me what town this is?"

"Why, London, to be sure!" replied the boy.

"Intelligent boy that," thought Mr. de Valera, rubbing his hands. "London, eh! London in England?"

"Yes, sir, in England right enough," said the boy.

"Ha! ha!" said Mr. de Valera, "and in the British Empire, eh?"

"Yes, sir, in the British Empire."

"Smart boy that," murmured Mr. de Valera, "in the British Empire, eh, the dear old Empire, never broken up yet I'll be bound?"

"No sir, never broken up."

"Then, here's a shilling for you. Now then, do you know the spot where they keep the Irish land annuities?"

"Oh, yes sir. Right around the corner. Commissioners of the National Debt. My eye! Do I know it? I saw a whole big bundle of them in the window yesterday. Christmas sale, sir."

"Do you think if I gave you some money you would go and buy me some?"

"How many do you want?"

"All they have!" said Mr. de Valera, "the whole lot. Here," he continued, throwing a tied-up bundle out of the window, "there's a couple of million pounds. Buy the annuities, call a cab and bring them back here and I'll give you an Irish Free State Terminable Debenture. Off you go now, like a shot."

Off like a shot! He would have been a quick hand with a gun who could have got a shot off half as fast.

When the boy came back with the Land Annuities, - and they filled the whole cab, - Mr. de Valera was standing fully dressed on the steps, his genial face beaming with benevolence.

"Right, my boy," he said as he handed the little fellow a 1975 debenture.

"Now then, cabby, in with those annuities into the hall here, smartly now, and I'll give you a Free State Consolidated Loan Coupon for 1981."

"My hat," said the cabman.

"I'll fill it with annuities, if you like," said Mr. de Valera, and they both roared.

"Comic fellow the cabman," thought Mr. de Valera, "genuine, hearty English spirit." "Now then, my man," he said, when the debentures were piled up in the hall, - and they filled one side of it, "do you think you know the way to drive me to Buckingham Palace?"

"Buckingham Palace!" exclaimed the man, "do I know it. Why I drove the King there last night!"

"Good! Then off we go."

"But they'll never let you in at this hour, sir," said the cabman, "it's too early."

"Won't they," chuckled Mr. de Valera as he got into the cab, "you just drive up and ring the bell and say that I've come to take the Oath of Allegiance!"

Ever after that Mr. de Valera was a better and nobler man, a kinder father, an easier uncle and a more religious pew-holder. Often in his old age he used to say: "It is nobler and wiser to perform a good action when you can than wait till you have to."

III
CHRISTMAS IN THE CASUAL WARD

This dear old story of Christmas is laid in and around a great London hospital. There has been a street accident on Christmas morning, and - but let the story speak for itself, with only the preliminary explanation that if Mahatma Gandhi never was in London at Christmas time, he might easily have been there.

The pathetic figure on the little stretcher was carried up the steps of the great hospital.

"What is it?" asked the group of people who had gathered about the entrance.

"Street accident," said the policeman (he was of course a burly policeman), "poor chap."

"Christmas too," said the doorman, "hard luck."

(The doorman had little ones of his own at home.)

"Is he much hurt?" asked a sympathetic bystander. (The unsympathetic ones hadn't thought of this question.)

"Can't live, I heard 'em say," said the policeman, "knocked down by a dray, I understand."

"I saw it happen," said a woman in the crowd. "Can't say it was the drayman's fault either, the little chap didn't seem to know where he was going - kind of dazed like, queer in his mind and talking to himself. Wasn't a white man, either, more like a Canadian or something."

Upstairs in the ward, a little group of nurses and interns stood about the bed on which lay the pathetic little figure. They were waiting for the great specialist who had been hurriedly summoned.

"Yes, once," said the patient, sitting half up. "At least that was what I had thirty years ago. It was a real English Christmas dinner, - " he seemed to gather annimation as he spoke - " we had turkey, - "

"and cranberry sauce?" laughed Sir Magnus, -

"Yes, and mashed potatoes."

"And plum pudding?"

"Oh, yes, yes, plum pudding, all on fire with brandy, and raisins and...

"You see," said the great specialist, turning to the little group, "it is simply a case of malnutrition, of underfeeding. If you young students," he added almost severely, "would only read a little old-fashioned Christmas literature, instead of sticking your heads into books of diagnosis, you would know that underfeeding is the cause, not only of all the street accidents, but of half the troubles of the world. This poor fellow - Gandhi is your name isn't it - is merely underfed: all the trouble came from that."

Half an hour after, Mahatma Gandhi, propped up in bed, a napkin at his neck, a tray in front of him, devoured wing after wing after wing of the turkey in front of him. Half a month after that he weighed two hundred and fifty pounds.

Half a year after that, India became free (to take effect A.D. 3000). Its liberator always used to say: "It is better my people give up swarai, sutteo, thuggee, and stick to things like Bombay Duck, Chutney, and Chile Con Carne, where you know what you are getting."

IV
THE UNCLE FROM AMERICA

Here is another familiar type of Christmas story that needs political application. It is called The Uncle From America, and is known in France as 'L'Oncle d'Amerique'. In this story, the uncle of a certain family is supposed to have gone away to America, years and years ago, - so long ago that his relations have lost all track of him. In reality, he has made a great fortune, but they do not know it. The family themselves have had exactly the opposite fate. They have sunk from affluence to poverty, their home has been mortgaged, and the mortgage has fallen due, as mortgages always do in fiction, on Christmas Eve, -
    And then, - well, every one knows what happens. But here is the political and international version of it.

The fatal evening had come. There was no help, no hope. The mortgage had fallen due. Tonight it would be foreclosed and Europa House, the fine old property that had come down for centuries must go under the hammer.
    Good old squire John Bull, the senior member of the family, restlessly paced the library floor, pausing at intervals to speak with a fair haired

gentleman who sat in an arm chair, his good humoured countenance [MISS-ING] by an expression of utter dejection.

"It's too damn bad, Fritz," said John Bull, "I wish the rotten business was over and done and the papers signed. Let the damn fellow take the old place. There's no help for it. You've no money have you, Fritz?"

Fritz shook his head.

"Not a mark," he said, "neither has Jacques nor Benito. Only paper and he won't take it."

"Damn his impudence," said John Bull, "but never mind Fritz, we'll stick it out together somehow. But here come the others, come in Jacques, come in Benito."

John Bull advanced to the door with outstretched hands with something of his old glad hospitality in his face, shaking hands with his guests as they arrived.

"Come in Jacques, - ah, and this is little Slovakia with you, is it, how are you dear? and this I suppose is cousin Polonia Corridor, - nay? but you have grown into a great girl! So cousin Ivan wouldn't come eh, - let him go to the devil in his own way - Angus, pour them out a glass of Scotch, it's there on the sideboard. Damn it, cousins, the old place is ours for half an hour yet anyway. Stir up the fire, Patrick, let us have a good blaze for the last one. Now then, you all know what the trouble is and why you're here, so we wont mince matters. This damn American fellow has closed out the mortgage. Well, - you've none of you any money, have you? what about you Benito?"

"Money!" said Benito, a dark Italian man, scarcely recognizable as cousin to John and Fritz, but resembling Jacques, "Money! millions and millions! I have kept telling you so."

"Then where is it?" said John Bull.

"I have told you," said Benito, "first lend me ten, - a hundred million lira, - and in ten years, - "

The assembled family broke into laughter.

"In ten years! mon cher Benito," said Jacques, "we are all like that. Oh, it is sad to think of it. Behold us, a united family, loving one another, and now, ruined by a stranger. Ah, if only Fritz had not made that sacred war!"

"Me make a war!" cried Fritz jumping up. "It is to laugh! You made it Jacques, you and Ivan."

"I make the war!" shouted Jacques, "you insult my honour do you. You shall answer, - "

"Gently, gently," said John Bull, "remember we are all cousins."

"I never made the war," said Fritz, his face distorted with anger, "I love peace. You Jacques, you and cousin John Bull here, - ."

"Damn your eyes, Fritz," said John Bull clenching his fist, I'm a peace loving man, but ... "

The room was instantly filled with angry tumult. But at that moment a butler announced at the door:

"The American gentlemen are here, Mr. Bull."

There was an instant silence as a tall man in a characteristic stovepipe hat and swallowtail coat, with a moustache and a long beard, walked into the room. He was followed by two others, evidently attorneys, who produced and spread out on the library table a bundle of documents, which they carried.

"Well, gents, and young ladies," said the Yankee, lighting a cigar without so much as asking permission or even removing his hat. "All here, eh, - quite a family party! Sounded from your voices just now like a real affectionate pow-wow!"

"Look here sir!" said John Bull striding towards the American. "Do the business you are here for, but your damned insults you can keep to yourself. I won't have them."

"And I too not," said Fritz.

"Nor me neither," said Jacques.

"All right," said the American quite unruffled. "I reckon money talks anyway. There's the conveyance laid out on the table. You get a discharge of all you owe and I take over Europa House and the grounds including the famous Concert Room and the Conservatory and the Moratorium. Now gents you can either put up or shut up. My pal there, Idaho Bill will either take the money or give you a pen to sign with. Which is it?"

The Yankee's manner as he looked at the assembled cousins seemed purposely and dramatically offensive. There was a moment of tense silence. Jacques' hands were clenched in anger: Benito's face was dark with rage, and Fritz's keen eyes glittered like steel.

But John Bull stepped towards the table.

"Cousins," he said, "there is no help for it. I am the oldest here. If there's been any fault it's mine as much as anyone's. I'll sign first."

And then a strange thing happened.

"Wait a bit," said the American. "I'll just see those papers are in the shape they ought to be."

He walked to the table, picked up the papers, carried them over to the fireplace, tore and crushed them into an indistinguishable mass, and threw them into the flames. Then as he turned round again, he took off his stove-pipe hat and false beard and stood smiling at the astonished family.

"Well, John," he said, "don't you know me now?"

"God bless my soul!" exclaimed Squire Bull, "Sam! Why it's Sam! Cousins this is your uncle Sam from America.

"Uncle Sam!" exclaimed everybody.

"Yes sir," said Uncle Sam, "back from America and back with a pile big enough to make the value of them papers look like two cents. Boys and girls, I've lived for years just for this. All the time I was working and making my pile. I thought of this homecoming to the old place, to clear up the mortgages, that I'd bought up one by one and pay back some part of what I owe. You and I, John, were kids together, Fritz, it was your mother taught me music. Jacques, I knew your pa. He gave me a statue once. Come cousins, fill 'em up to the health of the old house! We'll mend and repair it till it's grander than it ever was and your uncle Sam will pay the bill for the Reparations.

And as he spoke the Christmas bells rang out their glad message of Peace, including its' Economic Consequences, and good will towards Americans.

HOODOO McFIGGIN'S CHRISTMAS

This Santa Claus business is played out. It's a sneaking, underhand method, and the sooner it's exposed the better.

For a parent to get up under cover of the darkness of night and palm off a ten-cent necktie on a boy who had been expecting a ten-dollar watch, and then say that an angel sent it to him, is low, undeniably low.

I had a good opporunity of observing how the thing worked this Christmas, in the case of young Hoodoo McFiggin, the son and heir of the McFiggins, at whose house I board.

Hoodoo McFiggin is a good boy - a religous boy. He had been given to understand that Santa Claus would bring nothing to his father and mother because grown-up people don't get presents from the angels. So he saved up all his pocket money and bought a box of cigars for his father and a seventy-five cent diamond brooch for his mother. His own fortunes he left in the hands of the angels. But he prayed. He prayed every night for weeks that Santa Claus would bring him a pair of skates and a puppy-dog and an air-gun and a bicycle and a Noah's ark and a sleigh and a drum - altogether about a hundred and fifty dollars' worth of stuff.

I went into Hoodoo's room quite early Christmas morning. I had an idea that the scene would be interesting. I woke him up and he sat up in bed, his eyes glistening with radiant expectation, and began hauling things out of his stocking.

The first parcel was bulky; it was done up quite loosely and had an odd look generally.

"Ha! ha!" Hoodoo cried gleefully, as he began undoing it. "I'll bet it's the puppy-dog, all wrapped up in paper!"

And was it the puppy-dog? No, by no means. It was a pair of nice, strong, number-four boots, laces and all, labelled, "Hoodoo, from Santa Claus," and underneath Santa Claus had written, "95 net."

The boy's jaw fell with delight. "It's boots," he said, and plunged in his hand again.

He began hauling away at another parcel with renewed hope on his face.

This time the thing seemed like a little round box. Hoodoo tore the paper off it with a feverish hand. He shook it; something rattled inside.

"It's a watch and chain! It's a watch and chain!" he shouted. Then he pulled the lid off.

And was it a watch and chain? No. It was a box of nice, brand-new celluloid collars, a dozen of them all alike and all his own size.

The boy was so pleased that you could see his face crack up with pleasure.

He waited a few minutes until his intense joy subsided. Then he tried again.

This time the packet was long and hard. It resisted the touch and had a sort of funnel shape.

"It's a toy pistol!" said the boy, trembling with excitement. "Gee! I hope there are lots of caps with it! I'll fire some off now and wake up father."

No, my poor child, you will not wake your father with that. It is a useful thing, but it needs not caps and it fires no bullets, and you cannot wake a sleeping man with a tooth-brush. Yes, it was a tooth-brush - a regular beauty, pure bone all through, and ticketed with a little paper, "Hoodoo, from Santa Claus."

Again the expression of intense joy passed over the boy's face, and the tears of gratitude started from his eyes. He wiped them away with his tooth-brush and passed on.

The next packet was much larger and evidently contained something soft and bulky. It had been too long to go into the stocking and was tied outside.

"I wonder what this is," Hoodoo mused, half afraid to open it. Then his heart gave a great leap, and he forgot all his other presents in the anticipation of this one. "It's the drum, all wrapped up!"

Drum nothing! It was pants - a pair of the nicest little short pants - yellowish-brown short pants - with dear little stripes of colour running across both ways, and here again Santa Claus had written, "Hoodoo, from Santa Claus, one fort net."

But there was something wrapped up in it. Oh, yes! There was a pair of braces wrapped up in it, braces with a little steel sliding thing so that you could slide your pants up to your neck, if you wanted to.

The boy gave a dry sob of satisfaction. Then he took out his last present. "It's a book," he said, as he unwrapped it. "I wonder if it is fairy stories or adventures. Oh, I hope it's adventures! I'll read it all morning."

No, Hoodoo, it was not precisely adventures. It was a small family Bible. Hoodoo had not seen all his presents, and he arose and dressed. But he still had the fun of playing with his toys. That is always the chief delight of Christmas morning.

First he played with his tooth-brush. He got a whole lot of water and brushed all his teeth with it. This was huge.

Then he played with his collars. He had no end of fun with them, taking them all out one by one and swearing at them, and then putting them back and swearing at the whole lot together.

The next toy was his pants. He had immense fun there, putting them on and taking them off again, and then trying to guess which side was which by merely looking at them.

After that he took his book and read some adventures called "Genesis" till breakfast-time.

Then he went downstairs and kissed his father and mother. His father was smoking a cigar, and his mother had her new brooch on. Hoodoo's face was thoughtful, and a light seemed to have broken in upon his mind. Indeed, I think it altogether likely that next Christmas he will hang on to his own money and take chances on what the angels bring.

A CHRISTMAS EXAMINATION

With every revolving year - and the poets and the physicists agree that they do revolve - I am struck with the strange inconsistency of the words "Christmas Examination". Here on the other hand is Christmas, good, glad, old season with its holly berries and its lighted candles and its little children dancing in a world of magic round a glittering tree; Christmas with its fabled Santa Claus defying our modern civilization by squeezing his way down the galvanized iron pipe of a gas grate; Christmas with the sleighbells all ajingle, with bright snow in the streets, with the church bells ringing on a week day and such a crisp gladness in the air that even the angular faces of university professors are softened out into something approaching human kindliness.

Here, I say, on the one hand is Christmas.

And here on the other hand are Examinations with their sleepless nights and their fevered days, with crazy questions and crooked answers, set with the calculating cruelty of the inquisitor, answered with the patient resignation of the martyr, or with the fanatical frenzy of the devotee who has swallowed his instructor's text book and gone crazy over it; Examinations with their hideous percentages, their insulting distinctions of rank, and paid for, in cold fees, with money enough to spread a Christmas banquet for the whole university.

Here is Christmas and here are the Examinations. And the two won't go together.

We can't alter Christmas. We've had it nearly two thousand years now.

In a changing world its lights glimmer through the falling snow as a quiet beacon on things that alter not. It stands there fixed as a very saturnalia of good deeds, a reckless outbreak of licensed benevolence, with its loosened pocket books and smiling faces, just to show us on one day of the year what we might be on the other three hundred and sixty-four - stands a moment and then passes, leaving us to button about us again our little suit of protective selfishness with nothing but a memory to keep us warm inside.

Christmas we cannot alter. But the Examinations, we can. Why not? Why will not some theorist in education tell us how we can infuse into the Christmas examinations something of the spirit of the season that gives them birth? Can we not break down something of these rigid regulations that every candidate reads shuddering in the printed instructions on his examination book? Can we not so estimate our percentages and frame our questions?...

And when I had written thus far the whole idea of the thing broke upon me with the floodlight of discovery. Of course, nothing simpler; I reached out my hand and drew to me the hideous code of the examination regulations. I read it over with a shudder. Is it possible that for fifty years this university has tolerated such a flat violation of every rule of Christmas behaviour? I saw at once how, not only the regulations, but the very examination papers themselves ought to be so altered that the old malicious spirit might be driven right out of them and Christmas come to its own again even in an examination hall.

Here is the way it is done: -

REGULATIONS FOR CHRISTMAS EXAMINATIONS

1. Candidates are permitted, nay they are encouraged, to enter the examination hall half an hour after the examination has begun, and to leave it, re-enter it, walk across it, jump across it, roll round in it, lie down in it, tear their clothes, mutilate their books and, generally, to make themselves thoroughly and completely at home at the expense of the Univeristy.

2. Candidates are not only permitted to ask questions of the presiding examiner, but they may, if they like, talk to him, sing to him, hum grand opera to him in whole or in part, use his

fountain pen, borrow his money, and, if need be, for the sake of order, request him to leave the hall. But remember that the presiding examiner is like yourself - a very human being and, if you had the advantage of knowing him outside the classroom, you would find him at this time of year one of the jolliest creatures conceivable.

If you could see him presiding over the little candidates around the Christmas tree in his own house you would amost forgive him that silly dignity which he assumes to cover his natural humanity.

3. Speaking or communicating with every other candidate, male or female, is of course the privilege of every student and the use of the megaphone and gramophone shall in no way be curtailed or abridged.

4. Students may either make use of the books, papers and memoranda provided by the examiner, or may bring in their own memorandums, vademecums and conundrums, together with such dictographs, gramophones, linotypes, stethoscopes, or any other aids to memory that they see fit to use.

5. The plea of accident or forgetfulness will, of course, be immediately received in the same spirit as given.

6. Five per cent will be accepted as a satisfactory standard, but all students failing to obtain it may be, and most certainly will be, specially exempted from further effort by a vote of the Board of Governors.

So much for the regulations. But of course, still more can be accomplished if the examiners will only frame their questions to suit the gentle kindliness of the season. I should not wish to show in any great detail how this is to be accomplished. That would be trespassing on the work of departments other than our own. But I may be allowed to point the pathway of reform by proposing a few specimen questions in representative subjects.

CHRISTMAS EXAMINATION IN CLASSICS

1. Who was Themistocles? (Note in italics): If you can't think it out for yourself, he was a great Roman general, or Greek, or something. The examiner doesn't know much about it himself, but Lord bless you, at this time of year he doesn't care any more than you do.

2. Translate the accompanying passages, or don't bother to, just as you happen to feel about it. After all you must remember that ability to translate a lot of Latin verses is a poor test of what you really are worth.

3. Pick out all the verbs in the above and parse them, or, if you don't like picking them out, leave them sticking where they are. Remember that they've been there for two thousand years already.

There! That's the way the Christmas examination in Classics is to be conducted. And in the same fashion one might try to soften down the mathematical examination into something like this:-

EXAMINATION IN MATHEMATICS

1. Solve the following equations - but if you can't solve them, my dear boy, don't worry about it. Take them home to father as a Christmas present and tell him to solve them. It's his business anyway, not yours. He pays the fees and if he can't solve the equations, why your family must stand the loss of them. And, anyway, people ought not to mind the loss of a few equations at Christmas time.

There! That's enough for the Mathematical examination. And as for the rest, you can easily see how they ought to be framed.

But just wait a minute before we come to the end. There would remain one examination, just one, that I think every student ought to pass at this season, though he may forget it if he will, as all the kind things of Christmas are forgotten all too soon. I should call it, for want of another name, an Examination in Christmas Kindliness, and I warn you that nothing but a hundred per cent in it can be accepted for a pass. So here it is.

EXAMINATION IN CHRISTMAS KINDLINESS

1. Is the University such a bad place after all?

2. Don't you think that perhaps after all the professors and the faculty and the examiners and all the rest of the crabbed machinery of your daily toil is something striving for your good? Dip deep your pen in your Christmas ink, my boy, and overstate the truth for your soul's good.

3. Are you not going some day, when your college years are long since past, and when the poor fretful thing that is called practical life has caught you in its toils, and carries you onwards towards your last Christmas - are you not going to look back at them through the soft haze of recollection, as to the memory of a shaded caravansary in a long and weary pilgrimage?

A CHRISTMAS LETTER

MADEMOISELLE,
Allow me very gratefully but firmly to refuse your kind invitation. You doubtless mean well; but your ideas are unhappily mistaken.

Let us understand one another once and for all. I cannot at my mature age participate in the sports of children with such abandon as I could wish. I entertain, and have always entertained, the sincerest regard for such games as Hunt-the-Slipper and Blind-Man's Buff. But I have now reached a time of life, when, to have my eyes blindfolded and to have a powerful boy of ten hit me in the back with a hobby-horse and ask me to guess who hit me, provokes me to a fit of retaliation which could only culminate in reckless criminality. Nor can I cover my shoulders with a drawing-room rug and crawl round on my hands and knees under the pretense that I am a bear without a sense of personal insufficiency, which is painful to me.

Neither can I look on with a complacent eye at the sad spectacle of your young clerical friend, the Reverend Mr. Uttermost Farthing, abandoning himself to such gambols and appearing in the role of life and soul of the evening. Such a degradation of his holy calling grieves me, and I cannot but suspect him of ulterior motives.

You inform me that your maiden aunt intends to help you entertain the party. I have not, as you know, the honour of your aunt's acquaintance, yet I think I may with reason surmise that she will organize games - guessing games - in which she will ask me to name a river in Asia beginning with a Z; on my failure to do so she will put a hot plate down my neck as a forfeit, and the children will clap their hands. These games, my dear young friend, involve the use of a more adaptable intellect than mine, and I cannot consent to be a party to them.

May I say in conclusion that I do not consider a five-cent pen-wiper from the top branch of a Christmas tree any adequate compensation for the kind of evening you propose.

I have the honour
To subscribe myself,
Your obedient servant.

CAROLINE'S CHRISTMAS: OR, THE INEXPLICABLE INFANT

It was Christmas - Christmas with its mantle of white snow, scintillating from a thousand diamond points, Christmas with its good cheer, its peace on earth - Christmas with its feasting and merriment, Christmas with its - well, anyway, it was Christmas.

Or no, that's a slight slip; it wasn't exactly Christmas, it was Christmas Eve, Christmas Eve with its mantle of white snow lying beneath the calm moonlight - and, in fact, with practically the above list of accompanying circumstances with a few obvious emendations.

Yes, it was Christmas Eve.

And more than that!

Listen to *where* it was Christmas.

It was Christmas Eve on the Old Homestead. Reader, do you know, by sight, the Old Homestead? In the pauses of your work at your city desk, where you have grown rich and avaricious, does it never rise before your mind's eye, the quiet old homestead that knew you as a boy before your greed of gold tore you away from it? The Old Homestead that stands beside the road just on the rise of the hill, with its dark spruce trees wrapped in snow, the snug barns and straw behind it; while from its windows there streams a shaft of light from a coal-oil lamp, about as thick as a slate pencil that you can see four miles away, from the other side of the cedar swamp in the hollow. Don't talk to me of your modern searchlights and your incandescent arcs, beside that gleam of light from the coal-oil lamp in the farmhouse window. It will shine clear to the heart across thirty years of distance. Do you not turn, I say, sometimes, reader, from the roar and hustle of the city with its ill-gotten wealth and its godless creed of mammon, to think of the quiet homestead under the brow of the hill? You don't? Well, you skunk!

It was Christmas Eve.

The light shone from the windows of the homestead farm. The light of the log fire rose and flickered and mingled its red glare on the windows with the calm yellow of the lamplight.

John Enderby and his wife sat in the kitchen room of the farmstead. Do you know it, reader, the room called the kitchen? - with the open fire on its old brick hearth, and the cook stove in the corner. It is the room of the farm where people cook and eat and live. It is the livingroom. The only other room beside the bedroom is the small room in the front, chill-cold in winter, with an organ in it for playing "Rock of Ages" on, when company came. But this room is only used for music and funerals. The real room of the old farm is the kitchen. Does it not rise up before you, reader? It doesn't? Well, you darn fool!

At any rate there sat old John Enderby beside the plain deal table, his head bowed upon his hands, his grizzled face with its unshorn stubble stricken down with the lines of devastating trouble. From time to time he rose and cast a fresh stick of tamarack into the fire with a savage thud that sent a shower of sparks up the chimney. Across the fireplace sat his wife Anna on a straight-backed chair, looking into the fire with the mute resignation of her sex.

What was wrong with them anyway? Ah, reader, can you ask? Do you know or remember so little of the life of the old homestead? When I have said that it is the Old Homestead and Christmas Eve, and that the farmer is in great trouble and throwing tamarack at the fire, surely you ought to guess!

The Old Homestead was mortgaged! Ten years ago, reckless with debt, crazed with remorse, mad with despair and persecuted with rheumatism, John Enderby had mortgaged his farmstead for twenty-four dollars and thirty cents.

Tonight the mortgage fell due, tonight at midnight, Christmas night. Such is the way in which mortgages of this kind are always drawn. Yes, sir, it was drawn with such diabolical skill that on this night of all nights the mortgage would be foreclosed. At midnight the men would come with hammer and nails and foreclose it, nail it up tight.

So the afflicted couple sat.

Anna, with the patient resignation of her sex, sat silent or at times endeavoured to read. She had taken down from the little wall-shelf Bunyan's Holy Living and Holy Dying. She tried to read it. She could not. Then she had taken Dante's Inferno. She could not read it. Then she had selected Kant's Critique of Pure Reason. But she could not read it either. Lastly, she had taken the Farmers' Almanac for 1911. The books lay littered about her as she sat in patient despair.

John Enderby showed all the passion of an uncontrolled nature. At times he would reach out for the crock of buttermilk that stood beside him and drain a draught of the maddening liquid, till his brain glowed like the coals of the tamarack fire before him.

"John," pleaded Anna, "leave alone the buttermilk. It only maddens you. No good ever came of that."

"Aye, lass," said the farmer, with a bitter laugh, as he buried his head again in the crock, "what care I if it maddens me."

"Ah, John, you'd better be employed in reading the Good Book than in your wild courses. Here take it, father, and read it" - and she handed to him the well-worn black volume from the shelf. Enderby paused a moment and held the volume in his hand. He and his wife had known nothing of religious teaching in the public schools of their day, but the first-class non-sectarian education that the farmer had received had stood him in good stead.

"Take the book," she said. "Read, John, in this hour of affliction; it brings comfort."

The farmer took from her hand the well-worn copy of Euclid's Elements, and, laying aside his hat with reverence, he read aloud: "The angles at the base of an isoceles triangle are equal, and whosoever shall produce the sides, lo, the same also shall be equal each unto each."

The farmer put the book aside.

"It's no use, Anna. I can't read the good words tonight."

He rose, staggered to the crock of buttermilk, and before his wife could stay his hand, drained it to the last drop.

Then he sank heavily to his chair.

"Let them foreclose it, if they will," he said; "I am past caring."

The woman looked sadly into the fire.

Ah, if only her son Henry had been here. Henry, who had left them three years agone, and whose bright letters still brought from time to time the gleam of hope to the stricken farmhouse.

Henry was in Sing Sing. His letters brought news to his mother of his steady success; first in the baseball nine of the prison, a favourite with his wardens and the chaplain, the best bridge player of the corridor. Henry was pushing his way to the front with the old-time spirit of the Enderbys.

His mother had hoped that he might have been with her for Christmas, but Henry had written that it was practically impossible for him to leave Sing Sing. He could not see his way out. The authorities were arranging a dance and sleighing party for the Christmas celebration. He had some hope, he said, of slipping away unnoticed, but his doing so might excite attention.

Of the trouble at home Anna had told her son nothing.

No, Henry could not come. There was no help there. And William, the other son, ten years older than Henry. Alas, William had gone forth from the old homestead to fight his way in the great city! "Mother," he had said, "when I make a million dollars I'll come home. Till then goodbye," and he had gone.

How Anna's heart had beat for him. Would he make that million dollars? Would she ever live to see it? And as the years passed she and John had often sat in the evenings picturing William at home again, bringing with him a million dollars, or picturing the million dollars sent by express with love. But the years had passed. William came not. He did not come. The great city had swallowed him up as it has many another lad from the old homestead.

Anna started from her musing –

What was that at the door? The sound of a soft and timid rapping, and through the glass of the door-pane, a face, a woman's face looking into the fire-lit room with pleading eyes. What was it she bore in her arms, the little bundle that she held tight to her breast to shield it from the falling snow? Can you guess, reader? Try three guesses and see. Right you are. That's what it was.

The farmer's wife went hastily to the door.

"Lord's mercy!" she cried, "what are you doing out on such a night?

Come in, child, to the fire!"

The woman entered, carrying the little bundle with her, and looking with wide eyes (they were at least an inch and a half across) at Enderby and his wife. Anna could see that there was no wedding ring on her hand.

"Your name?" said the farmer's wife.

"My name is Caroline," the girl whispered. The rest was lost in the low tones of her voice. "I want shelter," she paused, "I want you to take the child."

Anna took the baby and laid it carefully on the top shelf of the cupboard, then she hastened to bring a glass of water and a doughnut, and set it before the half-frozen girl.

"Eat," she said, "and warm yourself."

John rose from his seat.

"I'll have no child of that sort here," he said.

"John, John," pleaded Anna, "remember what the Good Book says: 'Things which are equal to the same thing are equal to one another!'"

John sank back in his chair.

And why had Caroline no wedding ring? Ah, reader, can you not guess. Well, you can't. It wasn't what you think at all; so there. Caroline had no wedding ring because she had thrown it away in bitterness, as she tramped the streets of the great city. "Why," she cried, "should the wife of a man in the penitentiary wear a ring."

Then she had gone forth with the child from what had been her home.

It was the old sad story.

She had taken the baby and laid it tenderly, gently on a seat in the park. Then she walked rapidly away. A few minutes after a man had chased after Caroline with the little bundle in his arms. "I beg your pardon," he said, panting, "I think you left your baby in the park." Caroline thanked him.

Next she took the baby to the Grand Central Waitingroom, kissed it tenderly, and laid it on a shelf behind the lunch-counter.

A few minutes later an official, beaming with satisfaction, had brought it back to her.

"Yours, I think, madame," he said, as he handed it to her. Caroline thanked him.

Then she had left it at the desk of the Waldorf Astoria, and at the ticket-office of the subway.

It always came back.

Once or twice she took it to Brooklyn Bridge and threw it into the river, but perhaps something in the way it fell through the air touched the mother's heart and smote her, and she had decended to the river and fished it out.

Then Caroline had taken the child to the country. At first she thought to leave it on the wayside and she had put it down in the snow, and standing a little distance off had thrown mullein stalks at it, but something in the way the little bundle lay covered in the snow appealed to the mother's heart.

She picked it up and went on. "Somewhere," she murmured, "I shall find a door of kindness open to it." Soon after she had staggered into the homestead.

Anna, with true woman's kindness, asked no questions. She put the baby carefully away in a trunk, saw Caroline safely to bed in the best room, and returned to her seat beside the fire.

The old clock struck twenty minutes past eight.

Again a knock sounded at the door.

There entered the familiar figure of the village lawyer. His astrachan coat of yellow dogskin, his celluloid collar, and boots which reached no higher than the ankle, contrasted with the rude surroundings of the little room.

"Enderby," he said, "can you pay?"

"Lawyer Perkins," said the farmer, "give me time and I will; so help me, give me five years more and I'll clear this debt to the last cent."

"John," said the lawyer, touched in spite of his rough (dogskin) exterior, "I couldn't, if I would. These things are not what they were. It's a big New York corporation, Pinchem & Co., that makes these loans now, and they take their money on the day, or they sell you up. I can't help it. So there's your notice, John, and I am sorry! No, I'll take no buttermilk, I must keep a clear head to work," and with that he hurried out into the snow again.

John sat brooding in his chair.

The fire flickered down.

The old clock struck half-past eight, then it half struck a quarter to nine, then slowly it struck striking.

Presently Enderby rose, picked a lantern from its hook, "Mortgage or no mortgage," he said, "I must see to the stock."

He passed out of the house, and standing in the yard, looked over the snow to the cedar swamp beyond with the snow winding through it, far in the distance the lights of the village far away.

He thought of the forty years he had spent here on the homestead - the rude, pioneer days - the house he had built for himself, with its plain furniture, the old-fashioned spinning-wheel on which Anna had spun his trousers, the wooden telephone and the rude skidway on which he ate his meals.

He looked out over the swamp and sighed.

Down in the swamp, two miles away, could he but have seen it, there moved a sleigh, and in it a man dressed in a sealskin coat and silk hat, whose face beamed in the moonlight as he turned to and fro and stared at each object by the roadside as at an old familiar scene. Round his waist was a belt containing a million dollars in gold coin, and as he halted his horse in an opening of the road he unstrapped the belt and counted the coins.

Beside him there crouched in the bushes at the dark edge of the swamp road, with eyes that watched every glitter of the coins, and a hand that grasped a heavy cudgel of blackthorn, a man whose close-cropped hair and hard lined face belonged nowhere but within the walls of Sing Sing.

When the sleigh started again the man in the bushes followed doggedly in its track.

Meantime John Enderby had made the rounds of his outbuildings. He bedded the fat cattle that blinked in the flashing light of the lantern. He stood a moment among his hogs, and, farmer as he was, forgot his troubles a moment to speak to each, calling him by name. It smote him to think how at times he had been tempted to sell one of the hogs, or even to sell the cattle to clear the mortgage off the place. Thank God, however, he had put that temptation behind him.

As he reached the house a sleigh was standing on the roadway. Anna met him at the door. "John," she said, "there was a stranger came while you were in the barn, and wanted a lodging for the night; a city man, I reckon, by his clothes. I hated to refuse him, and I put him in Willie's room. We'll never want it again, and he's gone to sleep."

"Ay, we can't refuse."

John Enderby took out the horse to the barn, and then returned to his vigil with Anna beside the fire.

The fumes of the buttermilk had died out of his brain. He was thinking, as he sat there, of midnight and what it would bring.

In the room above, the man in the sealskin coat had thrown himself down, clothes and all, upon the bed, tired with his drive.

"How it all comes back to me," he muttered as he fell asleep, "the same old room, nothing changed - except them - how worn they look," and a tear started to his eyes. He thought of his leaving his home fifteen years ago, of his struggle in the great city, of the great idea he had conceived of making money, and of the Farm Investment Company he had instituted - the single system of applying the crushing power of capital to exact the uttermost penny from the farm loans. And now here he was back again, true to his word, with a million dollars in his belt. "Tomorrow," he had murmured, "I will tell them. It will be Christmas." Then William - yes, reader, it was William (see line 503 above) had fallen asleep.

The hours passed, and kept passing.

It was 11:30.

Then suddenly Anna started from her place.

"Henry!" she cried as the door opened and a man entered. He advanced gladly to meet her, and in a moment mother and son were folded in a close embrace. It was Henry, the man from Sing Sing. True to his word, he had slipped away unostentatiously at the height of the festivities.

"Alas, Henry," said the mother after the warmth of the first greetings had passed, "you come at an unlucky hour." They told him of the mortgage on the farm and the ruin of his home.

"Yes," said Anna, "not even a bed to offer you," and she spoke of the strangers who had arrived; of the stricken woman and the child, and the rich man in the sealskin coat who had asked for a night's shelter.

Henry listened intently while they told him of the man, and a sudden light of intelligence flashed into his eye.

"By Heaven, father, I have it!" he cried. Then dropping his voice, he said, "Speak low, father. This man upstairs, he had a sealskin coat and silk hat?"

"Yes," said the father.

"Father," said Henry, "I saw a man sitting in a sleigh in the cedar swamp. He had money in his hand, and he counted it, and chuckled, - five dollar gold pieces - in all, 1,125,465 dollars and a quarter."

The father and son looked at one another.

"I see your idea," said Enderby sternly.

"We'll choke him," said Henry.

"Or club him," said the farmer, "and pay the mortgage."

Anna looked from one to the other, joy and hope struggling with the sorrow in her face. "Henry, my Henry," she said proudly, "I knew he would find a way."

"Come on," said Henry; "bring the lamp, mother, take the club, father," and gaily, but with hushed voices, the three stole up the stairs.

The stranger lay sunk in sleep. The back of his head was turned to them as they came in.

"Now, mother," said the farmer firmly, "hold the lamp a little nearer; just behind the ear, I think, Henry."

"No," said Henry, rolling back his sleeve and speaking with the quick authority that sat well upon him, "across the jaw, father, it's quicker and neater."

"Well, well," said the farmer, smiling proudly, "have your own way, lad, you know best."

Henry raised the club.

But as he did so - say, what was that? Far away behind the cedar swamp the deep booming of the bell of the village church began to strike out midnight. One, two, three, its tones came clear across the crisp air. Almost at the same moment the clock below began with deep strokes to mark the midnight hour; from the farmyard chicken coop a rooster began to crow twelve times, while the loud lowing of the cattle and the soft cooing of the hogs seemed to usher in the morning of Christmas with its message of peace and goodwill.

The club fell from Henry's hand and rattled on the floor.

The sleeper woke, and sat up.

"Father! Mother!" he cried.

"My son, my son," sobbed the father, "we had guessed it was you. We had come to wake you."

"Yes, it is I," said William, smiling to his parents, "and I have brought the million dollars. Here it is," and with that he unstrapped the belt from his waist and laid a million dollars on the table.

"Thank Heaven!" cried Anna, "our troubles are at an end. This money will clear the mortgage - and the greed of Pinchem & Co. cannot harm us now."

"The farm was mortgaged!" said William, aghast.

"Ay," said the farmer, "mortgaged to men who have no conscience, whose greedy hand had nearly brought us to the grave. See how she has aged, my boy," and he pointed to Anna.

"Father," said William, in deep tones of contrition, "I am Pinchem & Co. Heaven help me! I see it now. I see at what expense of suffering my fortune was made. I will restore it all, three million dollars, to those I have wronged."

"No," said mother softly. "You repent, dear son, with true Christian repentance. That is enough. You may keep the money. We will look upon it as a trust, a sacred trust, and every time we spend a dollar of it on ourselves we will think of it as a trust."

"Yes," said the farmer softly, "your mother is right, the money is a trust, and we will restock the farm with it, buy out the Jones' property, and regard the whole thing as a trust."

At this moment the door of the room opened. A woman's form appeared. It was Caroline, robed in one of Anna's directoire nightgowns.

"I heard your voices," she said, and then, as she caught sight of Henry, she gave a great cry.

"My husband!"

"My wife," said Henry, and folded her to his heart.

"You have left Sing Sing?" cried Caroline with joy.

"Yes, Caroline," said Henry. "I shall never go back."

Gaily the reunited family descended. Anna carried the lamp, Henry carried the club. William carried the million dollars.

The tamarack fire roared again upon the hearth. The buttermilk circulated from hand to hand. William and Henry told and retold the story of their adventures. The first streak of the Christmas morn fell through the doorpane.

"Ah, my sons," said John Enderby, "henceforth let us stick to the narrow path. What is it that the Good Book says: 'A straight line is that which lies evenly between its extreme points.'"

THE ERRORS OF SANTA CLAUS

It was Christmas Eve.

The Browns, who lived in the adjoining house, had been dining with the Joneses.

Brown and Jones were sitting over wine and walnuts at the table. The others had gone upstairs.

"What are you giving to your boy for Christmas?" asked Brown.

"A train," said Jones, "new kind of thing - automatic."

"Let's have a look at it," said Brown.

Jones fetched a parcel from the sideboard and began unwrapping it.

"Ingenious thing, isn't it?" he said, "goes on its own rails. Queer how kids love to play with trains, isn't it?"

"Yes," assented Brown, "how are the rails fixed?"

"Wait, I'll show you," said Jones, "just help me to shove these dinner things aside and roll back the cloth. There! See! You lay the rails like that and fasten them at the end, so -"

"Oh, yes, I catch on, makes a grade, doesn't it? Just the thing to amuse a child, isn't it? I got Willie a toy aeroplane."

"I know, they're great. I got Edwin one on his birthday. But I thought I'd get him a train this time. I told him Santa Claus was going to bring him something altogether new this time. Edwin, of course, believes in Santa Claus absolutely. Say, look at this locomotive, would you? It has a spring coiled up inside the fire box."

"Wind her up," said Brown with great interest, "let's see her go."

"All right," said Jones, "just pile up two or three plates or something to lean the end of the rails on. There, notice the way it buzzes before it starts. Isn't that a great thing for a kid, eh?"

"Yes," said Brown, "and say! see this little spring to pull the whistle. By Gad, it toots, eh? Just like real?"

"Now then, Brown," Jones went on, "you hitch on those cars and I'll start her. I'll be engineer, eh!"

Half an hour later Brown and Jones were still playing trains on the dining-room table.

But their wives upstairs in the drawing room hardly noticed their absence. They were too much interested.

"Oh, I think it's perfectly sweet," said Mrs. Brown, "just the loveliest doll I've seen in years. I must get one like it for Ulvina. Won't Clarisse be perfectly enchanted?"

"Yes," answered Mrs. Jones, "and then she'll have all the fun of arranging the dresses. Children love that so much. Look! there are three little dresses with the doll, aren't they cute? All cut out and ready to stitch together."

"Oh, how perfectly lovely," exclaimed Mrs. Brown, "I think the mauve one would suit the doll best - don't you? - with such golden hair - only don't you think it would make it much nicer to turn back the collar, so, and to put a little band - so?"

"What a good idea!" said Mrs. Jones, "do let's try it. Just wait, I'll get a needle in a minute. I'll tell Clarisse that Santa Claus sewed it himself. The child believes in Santa Claus absolutely."

And half an hour later Mrs. Jones and Mrs. Brown were so busy stitching dolls' clothes that they could not hear the roaring of the little train up and down the dining table, and had no idea what the four children were doing.

Nor did the children miss their mothers.

"Dandy, aren't they?" Edwin Jones was saying to little Willie Brown, as they sat in Edwin's bedroom. "A hundred in a box, with cork tips, and see, an amber mouthpiece that fits into a little case at the side. Good present for dad, eh?"

"Fine!" said Willie, appreciatively. "I'm giving father cigars."

"I know, I thought of cigars too. Men always like cigars and cigarettes.

You can't go wrong on them. Say, would you like to try one or two of these cigarettes? We can take them from the bottom. You'll like them, they're Russian - away ahead of Egyptian."

"Thanks," answered Willie. "I'd like one immensely. I only started smoking last spring - on my twelfth birthday. I think a feller's a fool to begin smoking cigarettes too soon, don't you? It stunts him. I waited till I was twelve."

"Me too," said Edwin, as they lighted their cigarettes. "In fact, I wouldn't buy them now if it weren't for dad. I simply had to give him something from Santa Claus. He believes in Santa Claus absolutely, you know."

And while this was going on, Clarisse was showing little Ulvina the absolutely lovely little bridge set that she got for her mother.

"Aren't these markers perfectly charming?" said Ulvina, "and don't you love this little Dutch design - or is it Flemish, darling?"

"Dutch," said Clarisse, "isn't it quaint? And aren't these the dearest little things - for putting the money in when you play. I needn't have got them with it - they'd have sold the rest separately - but I think it's too utterly slow playing without money, don't you?"

"Oh, abominable," shuddered Ulvina, "but your mamma never plays for money, does she?"

"Mamma! Oh, gracious, no. Mamma's far too slow for that. But I shall tell her that Santa Claus insisted on putting in the little money boxes."

"I suppose she believes in Santa Claus, just as my Mamma does."

"Oh, absolutely," said Clarisse, and added, "What if we play a little game! With a double dummy, the French way, or Norwegian Skat, if you like. That only needs two."

"All right," agreed Ulvina, and in a few minutes they were deep in a game of cards with a little pile of pocket money beside them.

About half an hour later, all the members of the two families were down again in the drawing room. But of course nobody said anything about the presents. In any case they were all too busy looking at the beautiful big Bible, with maps in it, that the Joneses had bought to give to Grandfather. They all agreed that with the help of it, Grandfather could hunt up any place in Palestine in a moment, day or night.

But upstairs, away upstairs in a sitting room of his own, Grandfather

Jones was looking with an affectionate eye at the presents that stood beside him. There was a beautiful whiskey decanter, with silver filigree outside (and whiskey inside) for Jones, and for the little boy a big nickle-plated Jew's harp.

Later on, far in the night, the person, or the influence, or whatever it is called Santa Claus, took all the presents and placed them in the people's stockings.

And, being blind as he always has been, he gave the wrong things to the wrong people - in fact, he gave them just as indicated above.

But the next day, in the course of Christmas morning, the situation straightened itself out, just as it always does.

Indeed, by ten o'clock, Brown and Jones were playing with the train, and Mrs. Brown and Mrs. Jones were making dolls' clothes, and the boys were smoking cigarettes, and Clarisse and Ulvina were playing cards for their pocket money.

And upstairs - away up - Grandfather was drinking whiskey and playing the Jew's harp.

And so Christmas, just as it always does, turned out all right after all.

A BLIGHTED CHRISTMAS

This, I fear, is going to be a very gloomy Christmas. If it were possible to conceal the fact and brighten the day up a little bit, I for one would have been only too glad to do so. But as it is, we had better call the day the 25th of December and let it go at that.

What I mean is that when we look about us we see hardly anything except trouble. Take for instance in the first place this very untimely and unreasonable settlement of the Irish Question. There are so many of us who can look back affectionately upon forty years of the Irish Question that we shall feel lost without it. It appears that henceforth there isn't going to be any Irish Question. Debating Societies will be wrecked for want of it. Dinner parties will lose half the sparkle of their conversation. It will no longer be possible to make any use of such good old remarks as "After all the Irish are a gifted people", or "You must remember that fifty per cent of the great English generals were born in Ireland". The whole thing is finished. Ireland has been given Dominion Status. What it is, no one knows, but they've got it, and now they have sunk from the high place they had in the white light of publicity, to the level of the Canadians and New Zealanders. After this no one will ever pay any attention to them. To my mind this new way of getting rid of trouble by conferring Dominion Status on it is an unfair way out of a difficulty. And the habit seems to be growing. It is rumoured already that the Government is going to confer Dominion Status on Mr. Bernard Shaw and the Borough of Poplar and on the Income Tax and upon the man who sees the first crocus in Kensington Gardens.

I understand that they are even thinking of giving Dominion Status to the United States. It is understood that Mr. Balfour, who is so hard to resist, has offered it to President Harding. It would have been accepted at once but for the fact that Mr. Briand claimed that any such offer must be accompanied by a permission to increase the French Fire Brigade by fifty per cent. So there the thing sticks. But in any case what is the use of trying to turn everybody into Canadians. It can't be done.

But the worst feature of it all is to have settled the Irish Question just at Christmas. There are so many of us who have been accustomed every Christmas to forgive the Irish and to pray for them and now all that we can do is to pray for the Hindoos and Adly Pasha and the new Help Yourself Movement of the Falkland Islands.

But that is only trouble number one. There are others and worse. This terrible fall of prices that is going on right and left is eating the heart of Christmas as it has been. Speaking personally, I shall find in it a heavy loss. For years before prices rose I used to send such things as neckties and braces to a long list of friends. I had started to send them braces at Christmas about twenty-five years ago. And if you once send a man braces at Christmas there's no way to stop. You have to go on until either he dies or you do. But when the high prices came and economy became a matter of patriotism, I simply said to my friends, "You won't mind, I am sure, wearing those braces I gave you last year until things fall a bit". Of course they consented. I admit that they no longer presented quite the same trim, well braced appearance. There was a saggy look about them, and a wistfulness in their eyes. They were waiting, I know, for braces to fall. Last Tuesday it was announced on the Stock Exchange that braces had fallen again to the pre-war level. I have sent out twenty-five sets of them. And at the same time the disastrous fall in razor straps, pen wipers, shaving pads, match holders, pipe lighters, neckties and corkscrews has set all the old machinery at work again. We are fairly caught in it. If we send a man a pipe lighter or a pen wiper this Christmas, we must go right on till the next European war. It is too bad to see the fruits of the great war squandered in this fashion.

Almost equally heartbreaking is the dreadful Movement of Disarmament. Of course we might have known what would happen if a whole shipload of British sailors and diplomatists and journalists, were exposed to the hospitalities of Washington. The British and Americans are both alike. You can't drive them or lead them or coerce them. But if you give them a cigar they'll do anything. The inner history of the conference is only just beginning to be known. But it is whispered that immediately on his arrival Mr. Balfour was given a cigar by President Harding. Mr. Balfour at once offered to scrap five ships and invited the entire American Cabinet into the British Embassy where Sir A. Geddes was rash enough to offer them champagne. The American delegates immediately offered to scrap ten ships. Mr. Balfour, who simply cannot be outdone in international courtesy, saw the ten and raised it to twenty. President Harding saw the twenty, raised it to thirty and sent out for more poker chips. At the close of the play Lord Beatty, who is urbanity itself, offered to scrap Portsmouth dockyard and asked if anybody present would like Canada. President Harding replied, with his customary tact, that if England wanted The Philippines he would think it what he would term a desiduum of consistent normality to give them away. There is no telling what might have happened had not Mr. Briand interposed to say that any transfer of The Philippines must be regarded a signal for a twenty per cent increase of the Boy Scouts of France.

But even as things were, the Disarmament went far enough to leave us more or less stranded. In the good old days, it was so pleasant to be able to put up huge scrolls in the parish church, with PEACE ON EARTH, GOOD WILL TOWARDS MAN, and then all start quarrelling again like blazes at New Years. But now, owing to this wretched fumbling of things at Washington there is going to be PEACE all the year round, and Christmas has received a staggering blow.

The outlook is pretty dark. In only one direction do I see light and that is over toward Checko-Slovakia. It appears that Checko-Slovakia owes us fifty million sterling. I cannot quote the exact figure but it is either fifty million or fifty billion. In either case Checko-Slovakia is unable to pay. The announcement has just been made by M. Sgitzch, the new Treasurer, that the country is bankrupt, or at least that he sees his way to make it so in a week. It has been at once reported in city circles that there are "strained relations" between ourselves and Checko-Slovakia. Good: and what I say is let us keep them strained. I have lost nearly all the strained relations we ever had so let us cherish the few that we still have. I know that there are other opinions. The suggestion has been at once made for a 'round table conference' at which the whole thing can be freely discussed without formal protocol and something like a "gentleman's agreement" reached. I say don't do it. We are being ruined by these round table conferences. They are sitting round in Cairo and Calcutta and Capetown, filling all the best hotels and eating out our substance. I am told that Mr. Lloyd George has offered to go to Checko-Slovakia. Stop him. It is said that Professor Keynes has proved that the best way to deal with the debt of Checko-Slovakia is to send them whatever cash we have left, thereby turning the exchange upside down on them and forcing them to buy all their Christmas presents in Manchester.

Don't let's do anything of the sort. Let us send them a good old fashioned ultimatum, mobilize all the naval officers at the embankment hotels, raise the income tax another sixpence and defy them.

If we do that we might get back the dear old Christmas that we are losing. As it is the thing is blighted.

THIS DISCOLOURED CHRISTMAS

I don't want to grumble, but I must say that prospects for Christmas this year do not look bright. The more I look at the world about me, the less I like it.

In the first place, there is altogether too much of this 'red' business abroad among us. The newspapers tell us that the Bolsheviks are planning a huge 'red' movement against Asia. I understand that half the factory hands in America are 'red'. Most of the freshmen students in the college are turning red, so we are told. There is a 'red' movement spreading rapidly in art and literature. Red editors are writing inflammatory articles for red readers. Redness is invading the home. Our cook took a red streak yesterday. The furnace man is red. A red grocery man throws packets of tea against our back door and a red iceman smashes our refrigerator with huge blocks of vermillion ice.

Now, personally I am getting thoroughly fed up with this redness. If things don't change soon I'm going to take a red streak myself. I give our cook fair warning, through these columns, that the next time she turns red, I'll bite her. I'll nip a piece right out of her, I am just in the mood for it.

And the postman, of late there has been a kind of red touch in the way he delivers my letters. I don't like it. Let him take fair warning that if he doesn't alter, I'm going to turn red on him myself. And it will be on Christmas morning that I mean to do it. Every Christmas morning, for fifteen years, he has come to my door with the letters and with the full geniality of the Christmas season blossoming all over him. And every Christmas morning I have come out to him, in my pyjamas and dressing gown, to give him a dollar. There was something in the sheer geniality of the merry fellow that used to get me every time. I have that kind of feeble mind that easily responds to the pleasant pretenses of Christmas. The thing always went to my head and I was willing to stand on the doorstep, in my pyjamas in a snowstorm, and to hand out a dollar apiece to the postman, the iceman, the milkman, the grocery man, the policeman, the tax collector and even the man that reads the meter for the Gas Company.

Now let them all take warning, they've gone red and so will I. On Christmas morning I mean to sit at the top window and drop heavy stones on their heads as they come along.

But I wouldn't complain if it was *only* the redness that is perplexing the world at this glad season. Almost worse than the redness is the new form of whiteness that has broken out. I mean the overdose of philanthropy that is being thrust upon us. I am, I trust, as good a philanthropist as any man. For years and years, every Christmas I have given fifty cents to the Protestant Infants Home, and twenty-five cents to the Salvation Army and, in each case, merely signed the gift as "a friend", without asking recognition or publicity for it. But the pace of philanthropy has become too swift. In my city, and in every other, there are 'tags' and 'drives' and whirlwinds every day. Only yesterday, I was caught up in a Help the Homeless whirlwind, that tore ten dollars out of me and had hardly lit when I was struck right in the stomach by a Save-The-Children drive for fifty dollars. I have tags all over me, as thick as meal tickets in a butcher's shop. I have put my name down for installments that reach beyond the grave. I am pledged to the support of Boy Scouts, Girl Guides, retired policemen, reformed drunkards, liberated convicts, invalidated teachers and expatriated Armenians. The thing must stop. It has got to stop. In the good old days, Mr. Rockefeller used to look after all this. What is he doing now? He did it and I gave my twenty-five cents as a friend! Why can't we get back on that basis now. I ask him fairly, why? But even the redness and the whiteness are only part of it. What troubles me still more is the universal blueness. I never saw the paper so full of gloom. Sterling exchange keeps sinking. Gasoline is rising. Wheat is shrinking. The coal is nearly gone. There is hardly paper enough left to last out six more Sundays. The workers won't work. The thinkers can't think. The women are in revolt and, meantime, the death rate, the birth rate, the poor rate and the tax rate are quickly eating us up. With all this universal redness and whiteness and blueness around us, I must say things never looked so black.

There is nothing for it, as I see it, but to move with the times and to be redder than the red, whiter than the white, and as blue as the bluest. In other words, be a blackhearted, red-handed, blue-headed Bolshevik and take a drive on one's own account against the first, principles of civilization.

But, before I do this, I am willing to make the world at large an offer. Would it not be possible, just for once and for twenty-four hours, to restore to this present Christmas Day of 1920, of the old pretenses of the past. Let us hush the social unrest with the singing of the Doxology. Let us pretend, if it is only for twenty-four hours, that there are no troubles in the world, no strikes, no high cost of living, no Irish, no Russians, no League of Nations. Let us hand round again to one another the good old presents that were the coin current of Christmas, before the days of motor cars and luxury. Let us have our pockets full of knitted neckties and sticks of candy and ten cent copies of Pilgrims Progress ready to give away.

If the others will do this, I will. I will be right there on my doorstep waiting with dollars in my hand. My neighbour, on his way to church, may throw a playful snowball at me, and every Protestant infant that passes shall receive, I swear it, a stick of candy.

Come, can't we try it for once?

Afterwards, we can all raise hell again to our heart's content.

THE CHRISTMAS GHOST

UNEMPLOYMENT IN ONE OF OUR OLDEST INDUSTRIES

The other night I was sitting up late - away after nine o'clock - thinking about Christmas because it was getting near at hand. And, like everybody else who muses on that subject, I was thinking of the great changes that have taken place in regard to Christmas. I was contrasting Christmas in the old country house of a century ago, with the fires roaring up the chimneys, and Christmas in the modern apartment on the ninth floor with the gasoline generator turned on for the maid's bath.

I was thinking of the old stagecoach on the snowy road with its roof piled high with Christmas turkeys and a rosy-faced "guard" blowing on a keybugle and the passengers getting down every mile or so at a crooked inn to drink hot spiced ale - and I was comparing all that with the upper berth No. 6, car 220, train No. 53.

I was thinking of the Christmas landscape of long ago when night settled down upon it with the twinkle of light from the houses miles apart among the spruce trees, and contrasting the scene with the glare of motor lights upon the highways of today. I was thinking of the lonely highwayman shivering round with his clumsy pistols, and comparing the poor fellow's efforts with the high class bandits of today blowing up a steel express car with nitroglycerine and disappearing in a roar of gasoline explosions.

In other words I was contrasting yesterday and today. And on the whole yesterday seemed all to the good.

Nor was it only the warmth and romance and snugness of the old Christmas that seemed superior to our days, but Christmas carried with it then a special kind of thrill with its queer terrors, its empty heaths, its lonely graveyards, and its house that stood alone in a wood, haunted.

And thinking of that it occurred to me how completely the ghost business seems to be dying out of our Christmas literature. Not so very long ago there couldn't be a decent Christmas story or Christmas adventure without a ghost in it, whereas nowadays -

And just at that moment I looked and saw that there was a ghost in the room.

I can't imagine how he got in, but there he was, sitting in the other easy chair in the dark corner away from the firelight. He had on my own dressing gown and one saw but little of his face.

"Are you a ghost?" I asked. "Yes," he said, "worse luck, I am."

I noticed as he spoke that he seemd to wave and shiver as if he were made of smoke. I couldn't help but pity the poor fellow, he seemed so immaterial.

"Do you mind," he went on, in the same dejected tone, "if I sit here and haunt you for a while?"

"By all means," I said, "please do."

"Thanks," he answered, "I haven't had anything decent to work on for years and years. This is Christmas Eve, isn't it?"

"Yes, I said, "Christmas Eve."

"Used to be my busiest night," the ghost complained, "best night of the whole year - and now - say," he said, "would you believe it! I went down this evening to that dinner dance they have at the Ritz Carlton and I thought I'd haunt it - thought I'd stand behind one of the tables as a silent spectre, the way I used to in King George III's time - "

"Well?" I said.

"They put me out!" groaned the ghost, "the head waiter came up to me and said that he didn't allow silent spectres in the dining room. I was put out."

He groaned again.

"You seem," I said, "rather down on your luck?"

"Can you wonder?" said the ghost, and another shiver rippled up and down him. "I can't get anything to do. Talk of the unemployed - listen!" he went on, speaking with something like animation, "let me tell you the story of my life - "

"Can you make it short?" I said.

"I'll try. A hundred years ago - "

"Oh, I say!" I protested.

"I committed a terrible crime, a murder on the highway - "

"You'd get six months for that nowadays," I said.

"I was never detected. An innocent man was hanged. I died but I couldn't rest. I haunted the house beside the highway where the murder had been done. It had happened on Christmas Eve, and so, every year on that night - "

"I know," I interrupted, "you were heard dragging round a chain and moaning and that sort of thing; I've often ready about it."

"Precisely," said the ghost, "and for about eighty years it worked out admirably. People became afraid, the house was deserted, trees and shrubs grew thick around it, the wind whistled through its empty chimneys and its broken windows, and at night the lonely wayfarer went shuddering past and heard with terror the sound of a cry scarce human, while a cold sweat - "

"Quite so," I said, "a cold sweat, And what next?"

"The days of the motor car came and they paved the highways and knocked down the house and built a big garage there, with electricity as bright as day. You can't haunt a garage, can you? I tried to stick on and do a little groaning, but nobody seemed to pay attention; and anyway, I got nervous about the gasoline. I'm too immaterial to be round where there's gasoline. A fellow would blow up, wouldn't he?"

"He might," I said, "so what happened?"

"Well, one day somebody in the garage actually saw me and he threw a monkey wrench at me and told me to get the hell out of the garage. So I went."

"And after that?"

"I haunted round; I've kept on haunting round, but it's no good, there's nothing in it. Houses, hotels, I've tried it all. Once I thought that if I couldn't make a hit any other way, at least I could haunt children. You remember how little children used to live in terror of ghosts and see them in the dark corners of their bedrooms? Well, I admit it was a low down thing to do, but I tried that."

"And it didn't work?"

"Work! I should say not. I went one night to a bedroom where a couple of little boys were sleeping and I started in with a few groans and then half materialized myself, so that I could just be seen. One of the kids sat up in bed and nudged the other and said, 'Say! I do believe there's a ghost in the room!' And the other said, 'Hold on; don't scare him. Let's get the radio set and see if it'll go right through him.'

"They both hopped out of bed as brisk as bees and one called down-stairs, 'Dad, we've got a ghost up here! We don't know whether he's just an emanation or partially material. We're going to stick the radio into him - ' Believe me," continued the ghost, "that was all I waited to hear. Electricity just knocks me edgeways."

He shuddered. Then he went on.

"Well it's been like that ever since - nowhere to go and nothing to haunt. I've tried all the big hotels, railway stations, everywhere. Once I tried to haunt a Pullman car, but I had hardly started before I observed a notice, 'Quiet is requested for those already retired,' and I had to quit."

"Well, then," I said, "why don't you just get immaterial or dematerial or whatever you call it, and keep so? Why not go away wherever you belong and stay there?"

"That's the worst of it," answered the ghost, "they won't let us. They haul us back. These spiritualists have learned the trick of it and they just summon us up any time they like. They get a dollar apiece for each materialization, but what do we get?"

The ghost paused and a sort of spasm went all through him.

"Gol darn it," he exclaimed, "they're at me now. There's a - group of fools somewhere sitting round a table at a Christmas Eve party and they're calling up a ghost just for fun - a darned poor notion of fun, I call it - I'd like to - like to - "

But his voice trailed off. He seemed to collapse as he sat and my dressing gown fell on the floor. And at that moment I heard the ringing of the bells that meant it was Christmas midnight, and I knew that the poor fellow had been dragged off to work.

WAR-TIME SANTA CLAUS

I once asked a Christmas Eve group of children if they believed in Santa Claus. The very smallest ones answered without hesitation, "Why, of course!" The older ones shook their heads. The little girls smiled sadly but said nothing. One future scientist asserted boldly, "I know who it is"; and a little make-strong with his eye on gain said: "I believe in it all; I can believe anything." That boy, I realized, would one day be a bishop.

Thus does the bright illusion of Santa Claus fade away. The strange thing is that it could ever exist. It shows how different from ours are children's minds, as yet unformed and nebulous and all unbounded, still bright with the glory of the infinite. As yet physical science, calling itself the truth, has not over-clouded them. There is no reason for them why a bean should not grow into a beanstalk that reaches the sky in one night; no reason why a dog should not have eyes as big as the round tower of Copenhagen; no reason why a white cat should not, at one brave stoke of a sword, turn into a princess. Are not all these things known by children to be in books, read aloud to them in the firelight just when their heads begin to nod toward bedtime and the land of dreams more wonderful still?

We have to realize that the child's world is without economic purpose. A child doesn't understand - happy ignorance - that people are paid to do things. To a child the policeman rules the street for self-important majesty; the furnace man stokes the furnace because he loves the noise of falling coal and the fun of getting dirty; the grocer is held to his counter by the lure of aromatic spices and the joy of giving. And in this very ignorance there is a grain of truth. The child's economic world may be the one that we are reaching out in vain to find. Here is a by-path in the wood of economics that some day might be followed to new discovery. Meantime, the children know it well and gather beside it their flowers of beautiful illusion.

The Land of Enchantment of the child - with its Santa Claus and its Magic Grocer - breaks and dissolves slowly. But it has to break. There comes a time when children suspect, and then when they know, that Santa Claus is Father. Worse still, there comes a time when they get to know that Father, so to speak, is not Santa Claus - no longer the all-wonderful, all-powerful being that drew them in a little sleigh, and knew everything and told them about it. Father seems different when children realize that the geography class teacher knows more than he does, and that Father sometimes drinks a little too much, and quarrels with Mother. Pity we can't keep their world of illusion a little longer from shattering. It's not Santa Claus only that fades out. It's ourselves.

Then at last there comes to children the bitter fruit from the tree of economic knowledge. This shows them that the furnace man works for money, and that the postman doesn't carry letters just for fun of giving them in at the door. If it were not that new ideas and interests come to children even in this dilapidation, their disillusionment might pass into an old age, broken-hearted forever as its farewell to giants and fairies. One thinks of the overwise child of Gilbert's Bab Ballads: "Too precocious to thrive, he could not keep alive, and died an enfeebled old dotard at five."

Yet even after disillusionment, belief lingers. Belief is a survival instinct. We have to have it. Children growing older, and their mothers growing younger by living with them, cling to Santa Claus. If he is really not so, he has to be brought back again as a symbol, along with the Garden of Eden and Noah's Ark. No longer possible as a ruddy and rubicund old man with a snow-white corona of whiskers, he lives again as a sort of spirit of kindliness that rules the world, or at least once a year breaks into any house to show it what it might be.

But does he? Is there such a spirit in our world? Can we believe in Santa Claus?

All through life we carry this wondering question, these tattered beliefs, these fading visions seen through a crystal that grows dim. Yet, strangely enough, often at their dimmest, some passing breath of emergency, of life or death and sacrifice of self, clears the glass of the crystal and the vision is all there again. Thus does life present to all of us its alternations of faith and doubt, optimism and pessimism, belief and negation.

Is the world a good place or bad? An accident or a purpose? Down through the ages in all our literatures echoes the cry of denunciation against the world. Sunt lachrymae rerum, mourned the Roman poet - the world is full of weeping; and Shakespeare added, "All our yesterdays have lighted fools the way to dusty death." Yet the greatest denunciation is not in the voice of those who cry most loudly. Strutting Hamlet in his velvet suit calls out, "The time is out of joint," and egotism echoes it on. But far more poignant is the impotent despair of those whose life has wearied to its end, disillusioned, and who die turning their faces to the wall, still silent.

Is that the whole truth of it? Can life really be like that? With no Santa Claus in it, no element of mystery and wonder, no righteousness to it? It can't be. I remember a perplexed curate of the Church of England telling me that he felt that "after all, there must be a kind of something." That's just exactly how I feel about it. There must be something to believe in, life must have its Santa Claus.

What's more, we never needed Santa Claus so badly as we do at this present Christmas. I'm going to hang up my stocking anyway. Put yours there beside it. And I am going to write down the things I want Santa Claus to bring, and pin it up beside the stocking. So are you? Well, you wait till I've written mine first! Can't you learn to be unselfish at Christmas time?

So, first I'll tell Santa Claus that I don't want any new presents, only just to have back some of the old ones that are broken - well, yes, perhaps I broke them myself. Give me back, will you, that pretty little framed certificate called Belief in Humanity; you remember - you gave them to ever so many of us as children to hang up beside our beds. Later on I took mine out to look what was on the back of it, and I couldn't get it back in the frame and lost it.

Well, I'd like that and - oh, can I have a new League of Nations? You know, all set up on a rack that opens in and out. I broke the old one because I didn't know how to work it, but I'd like to try again. And may I have a brand new Magna Carta, and a Declaration of Independence and a Rights of Man and a Sermon on the Mount? And I'd like, if you don't mind, though of course it's more in the way of a toy, a little Jack-in-the-Box, one with a little Adolf Hitler in it. No, honestly, I wouldn't hurt him; I'd just hook the lid and keep him for a curiosity. I can't have it? Never mind.

Here, listen, this is what I want, Santa Claus, and here I'm speaking for all of us, millions and millions of us.

Bring us back the World We Had, and don't value at its worth - the Universal Peace, the Good Will Towards Men - all that we had and couldn't use and broke and threw away.

Give us that. This time we'll really try.

WAR-TIME CHRISTMAS

fter all - it's Christmas. It may seem to us the most distressed, the most tragic Christmas of the ages - Christmas in a world of disaster never known before. But yet, it's Christmas. And we ought to keep it so as the old, glad season of goodwill towards man, and kindliness and forgiveness towards everybody. Notice, towards everybody - even towards Adolf Hitler. What? You say you'd rather boil him in oil. Oh, but, of course, I include that; boil him, and then forgive him boiled. So with all the Germans - I'd like to drown them all in the Rhine, and then forgive them and send the Rhine to the wash.

A tragic Christmas - and yet, I don't know. When I begin to think of it, I am not sure whether it is tragic. It is a Christmas of disaster, but what is that? That passes away and is gone. But for the things that do not pass away, the permanent forces in human life, perhaps this Christmas is to be for us the most ennobling, the most inspiring of all there have been since the first Christmas announced salvation to the world.

I am thinking here of what has been done in England - the steady heroism of a whole nation that has gone out as a new light to lighten the world. This inspiration from England may prove, and I think it will, the first guidance towards a new world.

And when I say England, I must at once explain that I include Scotland and Wales and Northern Ireland and, naturally, the Isle of Man. People are so touchy on this point, especially since the war began, that I should not wish to hurt any one's feelings. When I say England and an Englishman, to me every Manxman is an Englishman, and every Welshman a Scotchman, and both Englishmen. For what else can you say? You can't say "a British"; that's not sense, nor a "Briton" because that means an Ancient Briton, stained blue, and studying with an axe to be a qualified Druid. Let him stay in the mistletoe; we don't want him.

So in the sense I mean, we can say that the word "Englishman" has taken on for the world a new meaning. Some people saw it long ago. W.S. Gilbert, of Gilbert and Sullivan, showed it to us fifty years back in his immortal vese:

> For he might have been a Russian,
> A Turk or else a Prussian,
> Or an Ital-ey-an.
> But in spite of all temptation
> To belong to another nation,
> He was born an Englishman.

People thought at the time that this was meant to be funny, and laughed at it. But we see now that Gilbert was just stating the quiet truth and was laughed at for it, as humourists always are.

"He was born an Englishman?"... Who wouldn't be? And all the world is being reborn into that heritage - which is the real, the spiritual meaning of this Christmas.

For me, I must have it so. For I cannot let Christmas go. Christmas has always seemed to me a day of enchantment, and the world about us on Christmas day, for one brief hour an enchanted world. On Christmas morning the streets are always bright with snow, not too much of it nor too little, hard-frozen snow, all crystals and glittering in the flood of sunshine that goes with Christmas day... If there was ever any other Christmas weather I have fortotten it... Only the memory of the good remains.

Into this enchanted world I step on Christmas morning, to walk the street and meet and greet at once, it seems, an enchanted friend. God bless the fellow! How happy and rosy and friendly he looks, and he draws off his glove to shake my hand - rosy and handsome in his silk hat (why doesn't he wear it every day?) and his white neckerchief... He must be sixty if he's a day, but on Christmas morning he looks a boy again, and he and I are back to school together. I must see more of him; true, I saw him at the club yesterday but he didn't look like this; something grouchy about him, taciturn sort of fellow - but on Christmas morning I can see him as he really is... But I no sooner leave him than I seem to run into half a dozen like him; the street seems full of them, all silk hats and white neckcloths... and "Merry Christmas!" here and "Merry Christmas!" there... old boys hauling sleighs with little grand-daughters done up in furs... or with a little convoy of great-nieces and grand-nephews. "Merry Christmas, children." Upon my word, I hadn't realized what a pleasant lot of friends I had.

No doubt you feel the same enchantment as I do! And it follows you all through Christmas day - at the dinner with the enchanted turkey, with every one a good fellow, and every good fellow wearing a tissue paper hat... the dinner followed by an enchanted sleigh-ride... with old friends, and meeting new people as you go - and every one of them so delightful... the world so generous, so bright. And then somehow the brightness passes, the light fades out, and it is tomorrow. You are back in the dull world of every day - anxious, suspicious, every man for himself. Friends? Which of them would lend me fifty dollars - come, I'll make it five!

This enchanted Christmas always seems to me to be a part of that super-self, that higher self that is in each of us, but that only comes to the surface in moments of trial or exaltation and in the hour of death. The super-self is always within call, and yet we cannot call it. I don't mean here the thing called the subconscious self, that evil, inward thing that can take my sleeping hand and write upon a slate, that can tell me where I lost my umbrella, or through a psychoanalyst betray by my dreams that for years I have had a complex to murder my aunt. ... Not that hideous stuff; nor any of the "complexes" and "behaviours" and "reactions," the new hideous brood of the new Black Art. Oh, no, I mean something infinitely more open, more above-board, more radiant than that... that light that shines in people's eyes who clasp hands and face danger together... the surge of sacrifice within the heart that lifts the individual life above itself.

All lovers - silly lovers in their silly stage - attain for a moment this super-self, each as towards the other. Each sees in the other what would be there for all the world to see in each of us, if we could but reach it. "She thinks he's wonderful," say her mocking friends. "He thinks she's a lulu!" laugh his associates. She is a lulu, and he is wonderful - till the light passes and is gone. "All the world loves a lover" - of course; one can see easily why.

It is towards this higher self - not as momentary exaltation but as sustained endeavour - that this Christmas of disaster is calling us. "Come up!" it beckons. "You must. There is no other way. This is the salvation of the world - come!" ... And on the answer is staked all the future of mankind.

For this altered world is not like anything that went before. Think back, as all people even in middle life can do, to what the world was like while the World War was just a dream, the vague theme of a romance.

To realize this alteration, come back with me in recollection, to church together - to an evening service, on Christmas Eve. ... Quiet and dim the church seems, the lights low, and from the altar comes the voice, half reading, half intoned, and from the dimness of the body of the church the murmur of the responses ... Give peace in our time, O Lord ... Peace! Why, it was always peace! What did we know then of world war, of world brutality, of the concentration camp and the mass slaughter of the innocent?

The responses echo back ... because there is none other that fighteth for us but only Thou, O Lord ... but what meaning could the words convey? nothing, or little - just a compliment murmured in the dark ... Strengthen her that she may vanquish and overcome all her enemies ... yes, but what enemies had she? Only a few poor Metabeles and Afridis, and such ... Vanquish them? Yes, of course, but then teach them to play cricket and mix a gin-fizz, and be part of the British Empire and ride in a barouche at a Jubilee, and then go out and help us conquer more...

From plaque and pestilence and famine... The voice is intoning the litany now, the prayer for deliverance ... from plague and pestilence and famine, from battle and murder and from sudden death... and the murmured response through the church... Good Lord, deliver us... The words are old, far older than the rubric of the church that uses them, handed down from prayer to prayer, since the days of the Barbarian Conquests of Europe, when they first went up as a cry of distress, a supplication... But can the ear not catch, in this new hour, the full meaning that was here - the cry of anguish that first inspired the prayer... to show thy mercy upon all prisoners and captives... In this, too, in now an infinity of meaning, of sympathy, of suffering... and as the service draws to its close: While there is time... intones the voice from the half darkness, while there is time...

What? What is that he is saying - while there is time? ... Does it mean it may be too late...

Not if we can listen each of us to the call, the inspiration of this darkened Christmas... the call of our higher selves. Up! Up! We have no other choice. We've got to.

SCENES FROM A RENOVATED CHRISTMAS

The letters and extracts and the little scenes that follow below don't really need any explanation. They explain themselves. But as some people always like to have all the t's crossed and all the i's dotted, perhaps a few words are in order.

I remember that at one of my own inimitable public lectures a man leaned out from the gallery and called, "Louder and funnier! please." That is exactly my point of view towards Christmas. We don't make enough of it; or rather we catch it and lose it. At Christmas time there is a pleasant pretense, a general make-believe that we are all better than we are: and not only better, but merrier. How brightly we greet one another on Christmas morning! How transformed are our ordinary dull faces! How easily we rise above any of the petty annoyances of life. Hear us at our breakfast -

"I'm so sorry, I'm afraid the toast is cold - "

"Oh, that doesn't matter, I like it better that way."

"The poached eggs, I'm afraid, are not so good as they might be. Willie dropped his Christmas paints into them."

"Oh, that's all right."

See us, when we go to church, all bright and rosy -

"Good morning! Good morning! Glorious day isn't it. The snow is lovely isn't it! And the air like wine, eh? You must drop in and see us. We never seem to get together."

All day we keep it up - our super-self, the submerged part of each of us, far beyond our common reach - and when the magic day has passed, it drops away from us. We can't hold it. The strain is too great.

But the chief reason by which we cannot keep ourselves at the Christmas level is because our sense of values is all wrong. We, the people of western civilization have bred in ourselves, as the price of our advancement, an over-great sense of the future, an over-anxiety, an over-appreciation of ultimate purpose, an under-appreciation of immediate good. We are never quite free from the little cloud of anxiety that surrounds and follows each of us as a nimbus. Our mind is set with a background of crepe. We can laugh, but you have to thump us hard to get it out of us. An Ethiopian can laugh at next to nothing. In merry Abyssinia, I imagine, they have a good time all the time. For which we go and drop bombs on them, on the ground that they don't work enough.

Of all our intellectual equipment, the thing we ought to value most, the sense of humour, the liberation that goes with laughter - we value least. We live in a prison with a door opening into a pleasant garden, and never pass through it. The garden, indeed, is walled. But so pleasantly it is grown with shrub and blossom that the wall you never see. So it is with life and laughter.

There is a story in the Greek mythology of how Pandora, the first woman, was sent to earth by Jupiter in order to perplex and disturb mankind. Among other things she was given a box from out of which flew Envy, Hatred and Malice, and all things evil. But with them at the bottom of all was Hope, which saved mankind.

The story is all right; but it would have been far better if Pandora had had Humour in the bottom of the box - the "saving sense" of a joke, as the true salvation of mankind.

Now let us suppose then that in these closing days of the year Jupiter looks out again from Olympus and sees that Pandora's poor little gift of Hope has proved quite ineffectual to dry the tears of mankind. Inspired with a bight idea (he seems to have got a bright one about once every five hundred years) Jupiter sends Pandora out again, this time with a box filled with Distilled Humour, to shake and distribute throughout the world.

As a matter of fact, as any chemical scientist will tell you, we even have the preparation all ready for Pandora to use. There is a gas that is called by science, Nitrous Oxide, but nicknamed by those who know it in practise as "Laughing Gas". Take a whiff or two of it and the world all at once turns upside down into the jolliest place imaginable.

Suppose Pandora, at our Christmas time, shook the box out all over us! How marvellous! What a change at once in our politics, our public life, our society. Let us illustrate what some of the effects of such a Renovated Christmas would be, beginning with the mightiest in the land and working downwards. Let us break into the mails (who cares, in a renovated world, for a little thing like robbing the mails) and read some of the correspondence of the great. Ha! here is an interesting item right away:

I

THE RENOVATED CHRISTMAS MAIL

FROM the Right Honourable R.B. Christmas Bennett to the Rev. William Spirit-of-fun Aberhart.

Dear Arb,

Sitting here laughing over the late elections, I've been thinking over that Social Credit stuff of yours, and I think I can begin to see far more fun in it than I did at the time. Mackenzie King and I were over in the Chateau Laurier today talking about that "twenty-five dollars each" and we just laughed and laughed! The new Governor-General came in and we told him, and honestly, he laughed until we thought he'd die! He says you ought to go over to England; they're too dull over there; you'd have the whole House of Lords in a roar. Let's think out some more good ones!

Still better work could be done by Pandora, if she would sprinkle a double dose of Nitrous Oxide over Geneva. The result would be something like this in the Press despatches of the next day:

II

CHRISTMAS MERRIMENT AT GENEVA

Geneva *(Night before Christmas)*. Fashionable Geneva never turned out in greater force than it did last night to attend the Gala Performance of Mr. John Bull, the Famous Ventriloquist, with his Talking Dolls. The scene was indeed a brilliant one inasmuch as it had been decided to use the Assembly Hall of the League of Nations for the putting on of the Comic Show. As Mr. Laffitoff, the delegate from Russia, said, "How in hell can we make a better use of it?" To which the delegate from Siam, we are told, answered,

"Eh what, me too!" Roars of laughter greeted the introduction of Mr. Bull on the Platform by Signor Aloisi, who described him as a Reformed Prize Fighter now going in for Ventriloquism. Signor Aloisi said that he only wished his leader Mussolini could have been present to sing his famous song, "A Life on the Ocean Wave." The house simply roared with laughter. Somebody shouted, "What about Hitler!" and again the house rocked with merriment. Indeed the entire audience was filled with what may be called the Geneva spirit and refused to take any of the proceedings seriously.

Mr. Bull's performance was preceded by a negro (Ethiopian) quartet who gave a marvellously appealing rendering of: "Way down upon the Tsana River."

Signor Aloisi was so moved that he said he would like to drop a bomb on them.

Mr. John Bull's own performance as a Ventriloquist with his Talking Dolls, had already enjoyed such wide publicity as to need no detailed explanation. Suffice it to say that Mr. Bull was in tip-top form. His capacious person and the singularly wide spread of his legs, encased in the familiar corduroy and gaiters enables Mr. Bull to hold what seems an extraordinary number of dolls on each knee. Some of the spectators expressed the opinion that he had a doll for just about every country in the league. His performance is indeed marvellous. When Mr. Bull throws back his head, with his features absolutely immobile and his expression entirely serious, it is impossible to believe that the voice is coming from Mr. Bull and not from the doll.

"Now then, Tommy," said Mr. Bull, giving a shake to a little doll, more or less collapsed upon one of his knees, and wearing round its neck the legend, "Tommy Laval, the Bon Marche Paris - now then Tommy what is your idea?" Tommy lifted his head, or seemed to, and said "Sanctions" - while the entire house broke into a roar of laughter. "And now, Pedro" - continued Mr. Bull, still absolutely grave, and shaking another doll, "and how are you today?" The doll Pedro, which had a label "Return Fare paid to Venezuelo, Second Class," raised itself upright, opened and shut its eyes a few times with a wide blink and said, "I love Italy!"

The evening was brought to a close with a little one act play - "The White Man's Burden," played by the entire cast of the league.

Nor is it only at Geneva that Pandora might benefit mankind. If she were to fly over to Ottawa and shake out a little Nitrous Oxide on Parliament Hill, our papers might carry the record of it.

III
OPENING OF PARLIAMENT AT OTTAWA

The opening session of the Parliament of Canada last month presented a scene of general hilarity scarcely equalled since Confederation. The entry of the new Governor-General was a signal for all memebers to rise and sing.

Do you ken John Buchan, as he was the other day,

But he's now Lord Something - it's a word that we can't say.

Equal merriment greated the new Prime Minister, the members, both Liberal and Conservative, joining in the Christmas hymn of:

Hark the herald angels sing,

Glory to Mackenzie King!

The prime minister, Sir William, as he now is, addressed the house. Members, he said, would observe that since he had taken office he had conferred a knighthood on himself *(laughter)*. He regarded this as a pretty rich joke on his right honourable friend opposite *(roars of laughter)*. But he thought fit to tell the house that his knighthood would be the only one given: he himself didn't believe in them, in fact he abominated them, and nothing but his sense of humour had induced him to assume one.

We would now, he said, take up the question of the Canadian National Railway and what to do with it. *(uproarious laughter, in which the prime minister joined)*. He would inform the house that the deficit on the rotten thing seemed bigger than ever: it was bigger on the first of December than on the first of November and in his opinion it was nothing to what it was going to be *(laughter and shouts)*. Figures would be laid before the house to prove this: he himself couldn't understand them: but he didn't need to. He had now a professor in his cabinet who could do all that sort of duty work *(cheers)*. He, himself, was going to take another trip to Japan, or perhaps to Honolulu - anywhere where there was a little brighter life than here *(cheers)*. He said that the budget would be brought down presently - that is sometime - he himself couldn't make head or tail of it, but if members would only leave things alone everything would be all right. He ended - so far as the Hansard reporters could get his words in the tumult of laughter - by telling the members to go to Hull.

When Pandora had finished with nations and parliaments she might turn her attention to the world of learning and brighten up our colleges with a little laughing gas. No more angry recriminations back and forward! No more complaints of the students that the professors are senile! No more complaints of the trustees that the students are bolsheviks! Not a bit. Listen to this, as a result of Pandora's visit:

IV

CHANCELLOR CORRECTS FALSE IMPRESSION

A distinct contribution to what one may call the Christmas spirit was made by the Chancellor of one of the greatest Canadian Universities in a speech to the students before dismissing them to their Christmas vacation. The Chancellor said that, a little while ago, he had been wrongly reported in the press, or at least so it seemed to him now - in connection with a speech made by him in another university. The speech was made as a denunciation of the spread of socialism and communism in the Canadian colleges, especially among the younger professors and the more ignorant students. The Chancellor was certain that he never said this. He certainly could not have used the phrase "the more ignorant of the students." If anybody could show him any students more ignorant than the others were, he'd be glad to see them *(applause)*. As to communism, he said he couldn't get too much of it. Nothing was more calculated to brighten up our colleges than a little wholesome revolution. In regard to the professors, he was glad that some of them at any rate had a little touch of youth about them. He looked round, he said, at the bunch of them in his employ and they looked a pretty rickety lot. But he could assure his young friends that means would be taken to get rid of most of them *(applause)*. Last year quite a few died *(cheers):* with luck a lot would drop this year.

But - the Chancellor added - why talk of education in a college. He would rather say a few words about the big game between Varsity and McGill this year that practically settled the Rugby championship. He had seldom seen finer and cleaner play and had realized when he looked at it that what we need at our Canadian colleges is more fun and lots of it!

But this renovated spirit can penetrate into even darker places than colleges and parliaments. I can imagine it invading even the criminal courts, the unknown domain from the very thought of which most of us turn with a shudder. *I have a friend,* a Chief Justice, one of the best, the kindliest, the wittiest of men. So nature made him. Yet there he has to sit in his criminal court and send people into the dark. If he could give way to the promptings of his own heart, or if Pandora might drop into his court some of the Tear Gas of Laughter of which we spoke, how different it might be. Witness this:

V

SCENE: THE CHIEF JUSTICE AND THE BURGLAR

The Chief Justice, looking at his notes, "You are accused here it seems, of breaking into the house. Is that correct?"

The Prisoner, "Yes."

"And you broke in at night, why at night? Can't you see that that is what aggravates your offense?"

"I had to break in at night," said the prisoner - " in the day, the dog was there."

"Oh, there was a dog?"

"Yes, one of those infernal police-dogs."

"Ah, well" (said the judge) "that's different, I don't blame you for that. I hate those infernal brutes myself. I can quite understand that in that case you would come at night. But, look, you climbed up and got into this man's house, into his study, by a first storey window. That's bad. Why didn't you go in by the door?'

"I couldn't get in. I had a skeleton key but the door had one of those narrow locks you can't see in the dark."

"Those things!" (said the judge) "yes, awful, aren't they. I have one on my front door: simply impossible to find! Well, that makes that clear. You couldn't get in at the door so you climbed up to the window. Then you got in, it seems, and took his money off the table. Why?"

"I needed it. I'd been cleaned out at bridge the night before and either I had to have that money or I'd have lost my game."

"You play bridge?" asked the judge eagerly.

"Oh yes, every day!"

"So do I. What do you think of the three diamonds convention - I mean after trumps are led?"

"No use for it. I think it spoils the game. In fact I'm against any conventions at all."

The Chief Justice with enthusiasm. "Exactly, just my own idea. Now let's settle this other business. First, it seems you came to this man's house at night because the fellow kept a dog there all day, couldn't get in because of his wretched, unworkable lock, you climbed to his room, found him out and took his money off the table in order so as not to miss your game of bridge. It seems from the record that you are a college man, and this man I understand is not, but has made a pile of money in business. The whole thing seems clear now: The case, if there ever was one, is dismissed and if you have no other engagement will you drop down to the University Club and have a game. I'd like to try out what you say about the conventions.

And the Chief Justice, as he left the court, deep in thought, realized, that if you see the world with proper vision, you can understand everything and forgive everything.

And with that, a Merry Christmas and a Happy New Year.

PHOTO: DON STANDFIELD

AFTERWORD:
A CHRISTMAS IN CONTEMPORARY MARIPOSA.

For over ten years I have been living with the kindly mischievous ghost of Stephen Leacock, surrounded by the things that formed the substance of his life. His rambling nineteen room house, his books, his letters, his pictures - even his very voice on tape that drifts through the familiar rooms as he narrates a whimsical tale.

The Stephen Leacock Home has been a literary shrine for thirty years. The restored mansion, its lawns and gardens and lakeside vistas lying in the summer sun, are familiar to thousands of annual visitors. Although Leacock built this as a summer home for his family and friends, it drew him back from Montreal throughout the year.

The Professor always comes up to Mariposa for his summer vacation and he generally manages to have a fortnight at Chistmas; he can usually snatch a week or two for the trout fishing in May and likes the break of a fortnight in early June for the herring fishing. Beyond that he has to content himself with the odd weekends. He's a busy man, he says so himself.

Leacock seems particularly near when the north winds blow, when the ice forms on Brewery Bay, and when the snow blankets the lawns and gardens. Christmas was a special time for Leacock and his friends. The fire crackles in the fireplaces, all nine of them, and Stephen entertains from his favourite chair with anecdotes of the Sunshine Town, or he mis-directs an original Leacock play, or he plays the convivial host for festive gatherings of family, friends and neighbours.

"Christmas With Stephen Leacock" recalls and illuminates the special season of winter and evokes the Christmas presence of a remarkable Canadian.

Jay Cody, Director
The Stephen Leacock Memorial Home
Orillia

PHOTO: DON STANDFIELD

109

ACKNOWLEDGEMENTS

We are grateful to the Stephen Leacock Memorial Home Board of Administrators for their approval of our use of the Leacock writings contained in this volume. The individual chapters are based on original material found in their archival files.

The publishers further acknowledge with gratitude the encouragement and cooperation of Mr. Jay Cody, personable curator at the Stephen Leacock Memorial Home, Orillia, and his able assistant, Mrs. Doris Medlock.

Prof. Ralph Curry, Pete McGarvey, Gary Lautens and John Robert Colombo were quick to respond with their Leacock expertise, once contacted by the publishers. Their encouragement and assistance have proven most helpful to this publishing project and are much appreciated. Further appreciation is due to the publisher's wife, Jane Gibson, for invaluable editorial input.

Finally, a special word of thanks to Barbara Nimmo of Michigan, copyright holder of all unpublished Leacock material. Permission to use articles to which she holds the copyright was graciously given.

Don Standfield is a freelance photographer currently living and working in Toronto. He has enjoyed a unique photographic career with assignments that have taken him to many regions throughout Canada.

PUBLISHER'S COMMENTS

As we approach the twenty first century, few publishers have the opportunity to present new works by an internationally recognized Canadian author. I feel privileged to be presenting to the reading public a collection of yuletide stories, some of them being published for the very first time.

Written during the interval between the two world wars, through the Great Depression and on into the deeply troubled times that preceded the outbreak of World War II, Stephen Leacock's observant eye and brilliant use of satire reminds us even today of the need to cast aside our differences and truly celebrate the meaning of the Christmas season, with the intention of carrying this meaning into our daily lives.

With bold pen strokes in the language of the time, Stephen Leacock often overstates to illustrate a point. He forces us to face the reality of our lives. In enjoying Leacock it helps to be able to accept the puncturing of one's heroes and even laugh at one's self. Such is the richness of Leacock humour.

Throughout the skillful drawing in of the famous and infamous, one can only speculate upon the names of those personalities that Leacock, if he were writing today, would take delight in incorporating into his writings.

Trained as an economist, Prof. Leacock was particularly attuned to national and international affairs and their impact on Canada. It is interesting to observe that as this book goes to print, the issue of free trade, delightfully lampooned in "Christmas Fiction and National Friction," is once more a major issue in the lives of Canadians.

Some readers may be reminded of the writing style of Dickens, some may associate the style with O'Henry. Whether you are an "old" Leacock fan or just being introduced to this world class humorist, you will agree that Leacock is Leacock.

A happy holiday season to all.

Barry L. Penhale,
Publisher